The Instrumental Music Director's Guide to Comprehensive Program Development

The Instrumental Music Director's Guide to Comprehensive Program Development

Michael J. Pagliaro

Published in cooperation with the National Association for Music Education
ROWMAN & LITTLEFIELD
Lanham • Boulder • New York • London

Published by Rowman & Littlefield
A wholly owned subsidiary of The Rowman & Littlefield Publishing Group, Inc.
4501 Forbes Boulevard, Suite 200, Lanham, Maryland 20706
www.rowman.com

16 Carlisle Street, London W1D 3BT, United Kingdom

Published in cooperation with the National Association for Music Education

British Library Cataloguing in Publication Information Available

Library of Congress Cataloging-in-Publication Data

Pagliaro, Michael J.
The instrumental music director's guide to comprehensive program development / Michael J. Pagliaro.
p. cm.
ISBN 978-1-4758-1287-9 (cloth : alk. paper) -- ISBN 978-1-4758-1288-6 (pbk. : alk. paper) -- ISBN 978-1-4758-1289-3 (electronic)
1. Instrumental music--Instruction and study. I. Title.
MT170.P32 2014
784.071--dc23

2014033667

∞™ The paper used in this publication meets the minimum requirements of American National Standard for Information Sciences Permanence of Paper for Printed Library Materials, ANSI/NISO Z39.48-1992.

Printed in the United States of America

Contents

Introduction

Teaching is difficult. Teaching in the arts is even more challenging because the subject matter is abstract and not easily processed by most individuals. When young students begin study, they are usually familiar to some extent with the subject at hand. Students speak a language: when they begin to study their native language, they have some conception, no matter how small or incorrect, of that language. The same is true with mathematics. If students are aware of things around them in quantities, a knowledge of some form of addition or subtraction is involved. For history, they have experienced a past, albeit a short one. For geography, they live in some location and so are aware of territory. All these experiences are more or less tangible. Living with them broadens one's skills and knowledge in those areas.

One might then ask, do not the arts fall into the same category? Students hear music and are exposed to art in various forms, such as architecture, pictures, paintings, and statues. Why not the same connection? The difference between the former and latter exposures is as follows: In the cases of language, math, history, and geography, students are everyday participants in those endeavors. With the arts, on the other hand, one's contact is in most cases detached. Most individuals are casual observers of the arts and hearers or recipients of music, whereas they are participants in language, handle quantities of items, are aware of a past, and are in touch with their own geography. Additionally, language is conducted by reading or writing using the alphabet and by speech, to which one is exposed from birth. Music is communicated through a series of dots and assorted symbols and transmitted through an instrument that serves as an appendage to the human body. Indeed, teaching is a tough job, and teaching music is even tougher.

The following pages are dedicated to making that job a bit easier and more gratifying by providing instrumental music teachers with teaching techniques, administrative and pedagogical procedures, and factual information on a broad spectrum of topics related to teaching instrumental music. The book is divided into three sections: The first section, chapters 1–3, discusses theories and philosophies of education. The second section, chapters 4–8, covers the many administrative obligations of an instrumental music director, including introducing new students to instruments, measuring students for a proper fit to the instruments they plan to play, and finding or creating content for lesson-plan enhancements to be used for the Common Core and Constructivist approaches, examples of which are offered here. The remainder of the book deals in detail with the business issues of being an instrumental music director. Included are suggestions for building a successful rapport with a music dealer, procedures for buying and renting instruments, and the processes for maintaining a school inventory of instruments in an effort to enhance and extend their performing lives.

For the convenience of the reader, some material will be repeated to prevent the need to turn pages back and forth, thereby losing focus on the issue at hand.

Chapter One

The Defined Instrument-Selection Process

A Pathway to Success

At the beginning of each school year, instrumental music teachers are faced with the task of assisting new students in the selection of an instrument to study. Some may consider this task just part of a day's work, but it is actually the most important undertaking of the year. For most students, the teacher is inaugurating what will be a relatively short-term learning experience. For some of the students, however, the teacher is launching a life-altering event that could ultimately lead to a career. The defined instrument-selection process described here is a protocol designed to facilitate the procedure used by a teacher and prospective student to select an instrument to study. Carefully evaluating a beginning student's physical, mental, emotional, and musical abilities before assigning an instrument pays off in a greatly reduced dropout rate.

At a teacher-student first meeting, the question inevitably asked by the teacher is, "What instrument would you like to play?" Certainly, this is the best place to start. Some students will choose an instrument that has captured their fancy, a choice often arrived at by virtue of their environmental experiences and exposure to music. Others will have no opinion but just want to be part of the program. What to do?

Exposure to music takes place with varying degrees of intensity ranging from casual, indirectly hearing it as a background to daily life, to actual direct experiences with instruments within a family, religious organizations, peer affiliations, or attendance at concerts. Choosing an instrument can be the result of a combination of those different life experiences. Often the choice

1

will be made based on an infatuation with an instrument for reasons of a personal nature unique to that student. There can also be the issue of a parent's desire for a child. For any number of reasons, some parents can have a particular instrument in mind that they would like their child to learn to play (I have one in the closet, I play one, my grandfather was a professional musician who played that instrument, I love the sound, etc.).

Music is everywhere. We hear it almost all day wherever we go. As we hear it, we are subconsciously processing those sounds that are appealing to us. When we are given the opportunity to select an instrument, we tend to make a selection based on those experiences. Perhaps we like the sound, it seems cool, it's the popular instrument of the era, or it was on television or the Internet. The issue then is whether the teacher should agree with the student's choice and move on with the program. The kid likes the flute; I can teach the flute; let him/her play the flute. That scenario can work and much too often is the game plan for the instrument-selection process. Unfortunately, it is not the best approach in giving guidance to what may be a very important decision in a young person's life.

Deciding on an instrument should certainly include consideration of the student's wishes, but there are a number of other factors that, when added to the equation, can result in a choice that could be more appropriate. Choosing the "correct" instrument for an individual is a pathway to greater success and all the personal gratification that accompanies that success. The use of the word *correct* can appear to some as stepping into dangerous territory. Who is to say what is or is not correct? Work with each student to decide on the virtues of that issue after walking through a comprehensive evaluation (CE) of the emotional, physical, intellectual, and musical strengths required for success in the study of a particular musical instrument. Armed with a completed CE, both teacher and student are better prepared to decide on a possible instrument or instrument category for the student to pursue.

The Comprehensive Evaluation: The leitmotif that should prevail while establishing a CE is the consideration for the student's wish for a particular instrument or inclination toward an instrument category. With that in mind, the process to follow for the CE should include all that is discussed in chapters 2–5. However, that content and the recommendations in those chapters are not absolute and do not necessarily need to be implemented in a particular order or at all depending on the particular situation. The optimal end product often results from the entire paradigm being followed, but doing so will have to be subject to the conditions afforded by the school district in which the program is being developed. When the final choice of instrument is made, the teacher must develop an individualized course of study that will capitalize on the student's strengths while teaching to the weaknesses found by the initial CE. When that curriculum is prepared, the student is ready to begin study.

Before there is an outcry about any form of discrimination or deliberate attempt toward exclusion in a program where an instrument is "selected" for study, let it be understood that the purpose of this exercise is not to exclude but rather to *include all interested parties*. The defined instrument-selection process does not select the student. The teacher in conjunction with the student selects the instrument that would be best suited to achieve success. The goal of using a defined instrument-selection process is to have an all-inclusive group of students who will have the best chance to achieve the highest level of success that their potential will allow.

Selecting the "incorrect" instrument can set the stage for just the opposite result. Frustration and failure are inevitable if one attempts to achieve what is difficult if not impossible because of a weakness in one or more of the elements necessary to play a particular instrument. If a student is trying to play an instrument that requires extraordinary strength in one area, be it physical or otherwise, and the student lacks that strength, that individual is more likely to underachieve. An awareness of a weakness provides a guide for the teacher to avoid those instruments that require strength in that area. Armed with an understanding of the entire student profile, the teacher is equipped to deflect the possibility of failure. Additionally, the informed teacher is better able to prepare an individualized curriculum that will foster the development of a student's strengths while making accommodations and preparing for improvements in any areas of weakness.

The Paradigm: The defined instrument-selection process begins with recruiting students for the instrumental-music program. Note that the recruitment is for the program, not yet for learning a particular instrument. A well-thought-out recruitment program in the school year preceding the year when study is to begin should include a publicity campaign featuring posters, announcements by the music staff, and demonstrations presented by the teachers and advanced students already in the program. These activities can then be followed by short performances featuring currently popular music, videos, text messages, and the use of other appropriate electronic devices to communicate the message of the wonders of playing an instrument. The messaging should be age-appropriate for the students being addressed.

Having succeeded in recruiting students to join the program, the next step would be to guide them in selecting an instrument. For this process to be of value, it will be necessary to have a system for identifying the physical, intellectual, musical, and emotional strengths and weaknesses of the potential student. Many students will have an instrument in mind as their first choice. A teacher who is charged with the responsibility of guiding beginners toward the instrument that is correct for them must be equipped with a practical, valid, logical process for doing so. The final choice should be the instrument that requires the strengths that parallel those of the student and that is most closely related to the instrument the student chose prior to the evaluation process. If they are the same instrument, great! If not, it will be the teacher's challenge to justify the difference in the mind of the student and, in many cases, the parent.

The evaluation process should include consideration for the student's interest and willingness to study the instrument selected. Willingness is of paramount importance, because if one is extremely qualified to play a particular instrument but not willing to do so, failure is likely. The student's strengths in conjunction with a willingness to use them will be the qualities that can lead to a positive, long-lasting relationship with an instrument. The willingness factor is very important.

A comprehensive evaluation to determine proper placement of a beginning student with a musical instrument takes time. It is, therefore, imperative that the process take place in the grade preceding that in which study is to begin. The first step could be to administer a standardized music aptitude test to all students in that grade in an effort to discover talent that is present and that could possibly go untapped. Bear in mind that music aptitude testing is neither discriminatory nor exclusionary but, rather, just the opposite. It serves the two very important purposes of defining extraordinary but dormant talent while providing an awareness of any areas of weakness in a student's musical mind. Armed with this information, the teacher is able to prepare an individualized curriculum that will remediate the weaknesses while capitalizing on the strengths.

One issue that has surfaced repeatedly over the years is the highly controversial one of using the results of music aptitude and IQ tests as part of a CE to precede guiding potential music students toward musical-instrument study. Assigning an instrument and a course of study based on anything less than a scientific evaluation of a student's potential is tantamount to a physician writing a prescription without first examining the patient. Such an act is unthinkable in the legitimate practice of medicine, yet music teachers commit an equivalent act quite freely when they allow new students to select an instrument without a full evaluation of what that student needs to ensure success. The practice of selecting an instrument on whimsy followed by a one-size-fits-all curriculum may well explain the excessive dropout rate in some school instrumental-music programs.

Chapter Two

A Brief Overview of Testing for Musical Instrument Learners

There is nothing so *unequal* as the *equal* treatment of students of *unequal* ability. —Plato, from *The Republic*

Determining one's potential to succeed in learning to play a musical instrument is a multifaceted process. Before the student chooses an instrument to study, a comprehensive profile can be developed to include an evaluation of the student's intellectual proficiency, music aptitude, physical size, strengths and weaknesses, cultural background, and emotional maturity. The red flag here is "cultural background." Let us address that immediately so the topic does not interfere with the task at hand. Cultures are different, period. Not necessarily better or worse, but they are different.

Addressing the differences from solely a musical perspective, one can easily identify the distinction between households where opera or rap are the prevalent musical experience. This is not an issue of which is better or worse. These experiences are just very different. The result may well be in the first case a child whose musical mind is conditioned to accepting a lyrical, bel canto auditory experience as being normal, whereas in the second case, one who accepts a rhythmic, nonlyrical, recitative auditory experience as being normal. If these students are given the same instrument and curriculum, the immediate position of acceptance by the two musical minds accustomed to very different concepts of what music should sound like will differ. They will require different curricula to achieve the same positive result. Therein lies one form of evidence that individualized instruction is essential to successful teaching and that developing an effective individualized curriculum requires a complete understanding of the gestalt of the student. Back to the topic!

Add to these evaluations a review of the student's personal interest and desire to play an instrument and the teacher has a solid basis on which to help select an instrument that will be consistent with the student's potential for success. The information for a model profile can be derived from standardized tests and one-on-one teacher/student interviews. The questions facing the use of a model profile are: How realistic is it? Is it doable? If yes, when, where, and how can it be done? Will it really help make a significant difference in the final choice? The answers to these questions can be found in a review of some of the testing programs currently in use.

I have addressed the various studies and commentary on testing in general terms, absent of footnotes and references. The goal is to introduce the reader to the existence of such information without turning the chapter into a lengthy discourse on the subject. An in-depth study of the world of testing would require volumes of text and many pages of footnotes. This is a job for doctoral candidates, not for this book.

Standardized Tests: By definition, all facets of a standardized test include questions, content, scoring, and testing protocols that do not vary. A group of individuals considered to be representative of a peer group is administered a test in a specific subject. Based on the results, norms are developed for each section of the test. All testing conditions are carefully controlled and results are evaluated for validity and reliability. When a standardized test is used, an individual's test score is compared to the norms established for that test.

Aptitude Tests: Aptitude tests are used to evaluate the innate ability of an individual to perform in a particular discipline. Such an evaluation presumes a lack of previous training. The test is usually given in anticipation of engaging in an activity related to the subject area of the test. Aptitude tests can be of a general nature, covering one's mathematical, verbal, analytical, perceptual, and general life skills, or the tests can be directed toward a single subject area. Although these tests can be used to identify and predict potential for successful achievement in a given area, the tests can also provide valuable information used to develop curricula that will capitalize on one's strengths while compensating for any weaknesses in an educational setting.

Of particular relevance to the subject of this book are music aptitude tests that are designed to identify one's strengths and weaknesses in the components that make up the musical mind. Among the components are rhythm, melody, pitch, tempo, and timbre. The Gordon Institute of Music Learning offers a series of music aptitude tests that include the seven components addressed below. Teachers who are preparing to engage in "the defined instrument-selection process" should evaluate the Gordon test series and other music aptitude tests to select one that will best fill the needs of the particular school program.

Music Aptitude Tests: Music Aptitude Tests (MATs) are designed to identify one's inherent ability to comprehend and to intellectually process music in the same way one does with language. The natural ability to think words with virtually no accompanying sound is present in most human beings. When reading these sentences, the reader thinks the words being read. It is also possible, although less commonly recognized, to do the same for music or musical sounds. Try thinking of a simple tune without making any accompanying sound: "Mary Had a Little Lamb," "Three Blind Mice," and so on. The process of thinking sound is possible for most thinking beings.

In 1975, Edwin Gordon, music education specialist and developer of the Gordon Music Aptitude Tests, coined the term *audiation* as a name for the process of *thinking* music as opposed to *hearing* it. In the process of audiation, the mind experiences cognitive recognition of the components of music without the sound actually being present. Those components are rhythm, melody, pitch, tempo, and timbre. The Gordon Institute of Music Learning offers a series of music aptitude tests designed to evaluate the potential of an individual who has had no music instruction. These are not achievement tests. The results of such MATs can be valuable tools in identifying an individual's musical strengths and weaknesses. Armed with this knowledge, the teacher is better equipped to develop an individualized curriculum designed to satisfy the needs of a student. Such a format sets a path for a program that is all-inclusive rather than exclusive, and where all students have the greatest likelihood of achieving their maximum potential.

The Gordon tests include seven components, divided into three categories: tonal imagery (melody and harmony), rhythm imagery (tempo and meter), and musical sensitivity (phrasing, balance, and style). The entire test series takes about three and a half hours to administer. There are also shorter versions of this test that are divided into three levels that take about twenty minutes each to administer. These shorter tests are the Primary Measures of Music Audiation (grades K–3), Intermediate Measures of Music Audiation (grades 1–6), and Advanced Measures of Music Audiation (college level).

The Gordon tests evaluate innate tonal and rhythmic aptitude. The test of tonal aptitude has the subject listen to a recorded sequence of two or five-note phrases presented in pairs. The two parts of the pair are either different or the same. The difference is only in the pitch, not in the note duration or timbre. The subject is asked to identify which pairs are the same and which are different.

The rhythm test presents the same format, but with either identical or slightly different second soundings. Again, the subject is to identify those that are the same or different. The pitches remain the same, and only the rhythm changes.

There are numerous other tests by other publishers that provide measurement of one's potential for music study. Again, the purpose of these forms of evaluation is to facilitate the development of an instrument-study program that will have students achieve at their maximum potential and will be all-inclusive rather than exclusive.

Skills Tests: Skills tests gauge an individual's ability to perform a specific task based on previous experiences. It is generally believed that skills tests do not measure innate ability. One must question that belief, for, although a degree of performance in a particular task does demonstrate previous experience, that experience must be supported by the individual's innate ability, that is, aptitude to perform in the area being measured. Logic dictates that one lacking the aptitude to perform a task but with some experience in doing it is less likely to outperform someone who has the same experience along with an extraordinary aptitude. The level of performance has to be the result of experience supported by an innate ability to implement that exercise. The reasonable conclusion is that skills tests do measure one's ability to perform certain tasks, but the tests can also to some degree be a measure of aptitude.

Achievement Tests: An achievement test, also known as a mental ability test, is a standardized test designed to evaluate learned information. These tests can be directed toward measuring any level of achievement in a given discipline, from basic beginning information or skills to those of the most advanced level. In addition to measuring the progress made in a particular endeavor, the results can also be used as a guide for placement into a program at a level commensurate with the subject's accomplishments. This procedure would help avoid the wasteful act of unnecessarily starting at the beginning of a process or at a randomly selected point in a program.

IQ (Intelligence Quotient) Tests: The relationship of IQ to achievement in the study of a musical instrument has been deliberated ad infinitum. A survey of studies on the topic leads this writer to conclude that there is a positive correlation between the two. If two people with equal aptitude in a given discipline but with widely divergent IQs engage in the same activity under the same circumstances, the person with a higher IQ is more likely to succeed than the person with the lower IQ is. Even in the absence of empirical evidence, it is not unreasonable to assume that one's level of intelligence affects learning in all disciplines. Of course, there will always be the exceptions.

IQ tests are standardized tests designed to measure one's ability to learn and understand information, to apply knowledge to solve problems, and to reason abstractly. The tests document and quantify basic intelligence. IQ tests have been the center of controversy for decades. Briefly stated, the challenge is that the terminology, word usage, and sentence structures used in these tests are, in many cases, specific to certain geographic regions and socioeconomic circumstances. Words that are commonly used in one social environment can have a different meaning or be virtually unknown in another venue.

The original intent of French psychologist Alfred Binet, the designer of the earliest IQ tests, was to identify students who were at the extreme ends of the intelligence spectrum. In so doing, he would then be able to provide special curricula on the lower end to provide for those individuals' special needs. Some tests currently in use by school districts are the Wechsler Adult Intelligence Scale for adults and older adolescents, the Stanford-Binet Intelligence Test for adults and children, and the Woodcock Johnson Test of Achievement, used to evaluate intelligence for individuals from age two to over ninety. These tests focus on measuring intellectual achievement and cognitive skills and are used as guides for the development of individualized curricula designed to maximize each student's potential for growth and learning.

In recent years, claims of discrimination against those on the lower end of the spectrum and elitism for those on the upper end have resulted in the use of IQ tests being challenged. The primary objection is that some consider the tests to be culturally biased. True or not, the fact that the question exists is enough to give using such tests special attention due to the possibility of unintended consequences. In spite of the challenges to IQ tests' validity and their usefulness, test results can be a valuable addition to the defined instrument-selection process. Advanced knowledge of the general intelligence of a student regardless of its cause is one of the best tools a teacher can have to avoid failure. If a student has an IQ that is below the class average, the teacher can be prepared to devise an individualized course of study designed to overcome any weaknesses. Conversely if, unknown to the teacher, a student has an exceptionally high IQ and is not presented with a sufficiently challenging course of study, boredom could ring the death knell for that student's interest in the subject being studied.

There are many reasons for not scoring well on any test, an axiom that can particularly apply to IQ tests. Do a Google search for "reasons for a low IQ" and you may find the results astounding. Among them are malnutrition, oxygen deprivation, sociological and environmental issues, emotional imbalances, and others. Although a low score on an intelligence test could be a red flag, the test in itself should not be the only quantifier of an individual's potential to succeed in instrumental-music study. Low score or high, almost everyone is able to achieve a reasonable degree of success on some musical instrument. There is an instrument for everyone. The trick is to find the right one. The results of such tests should never be used as a reason to deny entrance into a music program. Test results should instead be *one* of many tools to assist a teacher in developing a course of study that will best serve each individual.

The objective of the defined instrument-selection process is to establish a paradigm that will fill the needs of every student in a musical-instrument program. If the defined instrument-selection process is implemented prior to the start of study and individualized curricula are developed, the program will be equipped to provide for the needs of an all-inclusive student body. Regardless of intelligence level, everyone is qualified to study some musical instrument. Researchers such as Lynn Wilson-Gault (1989) and more recently Joanne Ruthsatz (2007) have concluded that there is a positive correlation between IQ and musical achievement. Such findings support the concept that using the results of IQ tests in conjunction with MATs will provide a teacher with information that can be used to develop individualized curricula.

Another dimension to the issue of IQ and music study is found in the separate studies of DeGiammarino (1989) and Gardner (1993), both of whom investigated the potential for music study by students who had various intellectually disabilities. One conclusion was that a student's degree of intellectual disability was commensurate with his or her level of musical achievement. In these studies, students who were profoundly intellectually disabled achieved more slowly than did those having higher IQs. These findings only serve to fortify the concept that individual evaluation of all potential musical-instrument students is essential to a successful program.

Emotional Intelligence Tests: Emotional intelligence (EI) can be a very important element in evaluating an individual's potential to succeed at any task. About a century ago, Charles Darwin postulated that emotional intelligence was needed for one to survive. Since then, studies have yielded a spate of conflicting information that seems to indicate that including EI testing as part of a profile for a beginning instrumental-music student would be of little value and may even be counterproductive. Research in the area of EI reveals a broad spectrum of results and opinions. Numerous testing formats and studies are used by some to justify what others consider unsubstantiated theories. It seems that the argument is far from over.

One definition of EI is the degree to which one is able to control one's emotions. A more popular perception of the subject divides it into the categories of *ability* EI and *trait* EI. Ability EI emphasizes emotions as the driver for an individual to deal with the travails of life. In this model, one can identify emotions, comprehend the subtleties of emotions, use emotions in intellectual endeavors, and control both negative and positive emotions so that they are used to an advantage. Ability EI can be gauged using standardized tests.

Trait EI refers to one's perception of the emotions of the inner self, quantified by the individual's self-evaluation. Trait EI cannot be correlated with traditional-intelligence measurement vehicles, since empirical studies show little correlation between the two.

How, then, does the teacher evaluate and document the student's EI in order to capitalize on strengths or compensate for weaknesses? The available standardized tests in this area are in many respects less than adequate. It therefore becomes the teacher's task to evaluate a potential student's emotional intelligence by observation and anecdotal analysis. The findings can then be included in the preparation of the student's profile in the form of an estimate of all the intangible, nontestable emotional characteristics demonstrated by the student during the defined instrument-selection process. An experienced, perceptive teacher using anecdotal observations should be able to gain enough insight into a student's inner self to make a significant contribution to the final profile.

Summary: Over many decades of teaching, I have come to believe that one's emotions—sensitivity or feelings and attitudes toward approaching any endeavor—are central to the potential for success. Attitude and passion can often trump talent. A less-gifted, inspired student can outdo a gifted, uninspired student. The opening paragraphs of this chapter asked whether the use of a model profile would be realistic, if it is doable, and, if yes, when, where, and how it can be administrated, and whether it will really help make a significant difference in the student's final choice of instrument. Does the time and effort required to administer tests justify their contribution to the cause? There is no shortage in both the quantity and variety of tests that might assist in developing a student profile. The fundamental question that must be addressed is whether using these tests makes a significant contribution to defining a student's potential. If the answer is yes, then which tests should be given priority? Teacher's choice! I have used a number of tests described here with great success, and I encourage you to begin the process.

Chapter Three

The Informed Approach

"Give a man a fish and you feed him for a day; teach a man to fish and you feed him for a lifetime." This ancient Chinese proverb has special significance for instrumental music teachers who strive to make their students independent-thinking, lifelong learners.

The "informed approach" is a protocol for introducing subject matter to beginning instrumental music students. New information is processed in an intellectual environment, that is, a "mindset" that is the product of each person's unique life experiences. New information is modified and interpreted to some degree from the learner's unique perspective. Using this informed approach encourages students to gather information, analyze it, and draw conclusions. The process fosters an understanding of how to use information in a productive manner. By doing so, learners can develop intellectual independence that will expand their interpretation beyond the original concepts and improve their ability to process information in all areas of study. Using this approach, as opposed to a teacher feeding a student information, helps develop in the student an inquiring mind that can be used throughout one's life experiences.

The informed approach requires that the teacher understand relationships among music, logical deduction, and the acoustic sciences. Applying these skills to the study of instrumental music accelerates the learning process, increases the knowledge base, and develops cognitive skills that can be applied to other studies. Students who learn that an *action* can achieve a *result* come to realize that when one operates a key, valve, slide, or string in a certain way (*an action*), a particular note occurs (*the result*). If the *action* is the correct fingering, the *result* is the desired note. When students attain an awareness of what is happening within an instrument that causes a note to sound a certain way, they develop better control of their instrument and are able to learn fingering through understanding and deduction rather than by rote. Simply stated, students learn cause and effect. If one knows how something works, it is easier to work it.

Fingering by Deduction, Not Instruction: After a student has learned to produce a sound on an instrument, understanding how fingering works can begin. The informed approach teaches fingering patterns in their totality as opposed to one note at a time. This process prepares students to find the fingering for any note without having to rely on a fingering chart.

The traditional introduction to fingering usually begins with a series of one- or two-note topics accompanied by simple playing exercises for those notes. This approach does not bring to light the fact that every instrument has an easy-to-understand structured fingering pattern that, when understood, significantly facilitates learning the fingerings for all notes on a given instrument as well as on almost all the instruments in that family of instruments.

String Instruments: For string instruments, understanding that notes produced on open strings can be changed to different notes by using a sequential fingering pattern is the foundation for learning fingering without the aid of a fingering chart.

1. Adjusting the length of a string using the fingers can raise or lower notes.
2. Depressing a string against the fingerboard with one finger in the correct place will raise the pitch one note higher, two fingers, two notes higher, and so on.
3. The converse also applies to lowering notes when releasing fingers.

Half steps, whole steps, and intervals can be addressed as the basic concept is developed.

Equipped with this knowledge, students are able to arrive at correct fingering by deduction rather than instruction. Fingering is learned by determining cause and effect, reasoning that in order to get a particular result, a certain action must be taken. Students must shorten a string to achieve higher notes or lengthen a string for lower notes. They now have intellectual control over the process instead of dependency on a fingering chart.

To avoid the challenges of bowing techniques, one should be introduced to the topic of basic fingering using pizzicato. Violins and violas can be held in the guitar playing position for the introductory lesson while cellos and double basses are held in traditional playing position. These positions permit the students to look at the fingering patterns, adding visual reinforcement to learning finger placement and interval concepts.

Students should begin by singing the first three notes of the G scale using the syllables *do*, *re*, and *mi.* Then, while the players are holding the instruments in the positions described above, have them finger and pluck those ascending three notes of the G scale by ear starting on the open G string. When they have achieved that with reasonable skill, have them do so in reverse, descending *mi, re, do.* When that exercise is successfully accomplished on the G string, repeat the same process on the D and A strings. Then have the cellos and violas play a duet on the C string followed by the violins and double basses on the E string. That sound combination will be amusing.

When the students are comfortable playing that sequence, encourage a session of improvisation by allowing the students to pluck away, aiming to play "Hot Cross Buns," "Mary Had a Little Lamb," or other simple tunes familiar to them. Aim toward creating a fun-filled experience based on the discovery of cause and effect.

Woodwind Instruments: All Western European woodwind instruments are constructed with a basic set of six tone holes on the front of the body of the instrument. These six tone holes are covered by the index, middle, and ring fingers of each hand. All the woodwinds with the exception of the saxophone have a thumbhole on the back. Tone holes covered by keys in other locations on the body complete the key system on the instrument. Understanding four basic principles of fingering on woodwind instruments will enable a student to determine the fingering for most notes without resorting to a fingering chart.

1. The actual sound-producing length of an instrument is the distance from the mouthpiece to the first open hole.
2. Shorter instruments produce higher notes.
3. Longer instruments produce lower notes.

As the player covers the holes in consecutive descending order, the effective instrument length increases and the notes get lower. As the holes are uncovered, the effective instrument length gets shorter and the notes get higher.

After the appropriate embouchure is established and the student can produce a tone on the instrument, introduce fingering using the following steps:

1. Have the student play the note that is open.
2. Have the student cover the first hole on the instrument. (In some cases it will be the thumbhole) This produces a sound that is one note lower.
3. Have the student continue to finger down the instrument by covering the holes in a descending pattern sequentially until all the holes are covered and the lowest note is sounding.
4. Have the student name the progressively lower notes based on the name of the first open note. Help with the accidentals.
5. Emphasize the fact that as the holes are covered, the distance the air travels becomes longer and the sound lower.

Through inquiry, analysis, and conceptual understanding, students discover the relationship of the *action* (covering holes) that must be taken to produce a particular *result* (playing lower or higher notes). When this concept is firmly established with the basic six open holes and the thumbhole, the lessons can progress to using side keys to alter the tones produced when any or all of the six open holes are covered. Covering the thumbhole when needed and then covering the six open holes one at a time in descending order from the top down will produce a descending sequence of notes. Depressing the register key or octave key with the thumbhole covered when needed will raise all notes an octave or on a clarinet a twelfth.

When the above exercise can be performed with some degree of proficiency, introduce a period of improvisation using the *do, re, mi* or the "Mary Had a Little Lamb" experience described above in the string-instrument section.

Brass Instruments: A series of open tones can be produced on all brass instruments without fingerings. With the exception of the slide trombone, all brass instruments use valves to produce notes other than the open tones. The slide trombone uses a slide. Using the following simple steps, a student can be introduced to fingerings by discovering the relationship of an *action* (depressing valves) that must be taken to produce a particular *result* (playing lower notes).

Depressing valves opens sections of tubing, thereby increasing the length of the sound-producing body of the instrument. By depressing valves, open tones can be lowered in half-step increments to produce the tones that exist between each open tone. The valves can be used individually or in combination, lowering an open tone by the following intervals:

> valve 1 = whole step or a second
> valve 2 = half step or minor second
> valve 3 = step and a half or minor third
> valves 1 + 2 = step and a half or a minor third
> valves 2 + 3 = two whole steps or a major third
> valves 1 + 3 = two and a half steps or a perfect fourth
> valves 1, 2, + 3 = three whole steps of a diminished fourth

To teach students how to determine fingerings for any valve instrument without using a fingering chart, have the students play an open tone that is convenient for them, and then apply the above principles. For the slide trombone, start in first position and move the slide down progressively, listening for the half- and whole-step progressions. In the case of the slide trombone, more attention will have to be paid to intonation and pitch discrimination because of the nature of the instrument.

A student who understands what *action* must be taken to achieve a particular *result* will be better prepared to discover the fingering for any note without relying on a fingering chart. This facility serves to reinforce self-confidence and strengthen playing dexterity.

Review: When the exercises just described have been successfully implemented and the students understand the principles by which they can achieve the desired *result,* students can produce their own fingering charts to illustrate their knowledge. Their fingering chart can then be compared to a traditional one, where students will see in print what they already know and have experienced.

Preparation for any endeavor is always desirable and essential. The time and effort invested in teaching how something works before teaching one how to work it will yield an exponential return. Understanding the principles by which notes change on an instrument empowers the player to progress through the learning process more easily while solidifying confidence in the actions at hand. "I know how it works, so I know I can make it work." On that basis, logic dictates that understanding the science and technology of a musical instrument can have the effect of engendering more rapid progress, a more confident performer, and greater facility with that instrument.

In light of this method of learning by understanding that an action can produce a particular result, one might justifiably conclude that this is a constructivist approach. Through exposure to a particular knowledge base and the use of that knowledge in combination with other directly related or indirectly related experiences, the learner formulates a series of conclusions. Information is perceived through the totality of the individual's experiences associated with the topic to ultimately draw new conclusions, learn new information, and apply that new information to the instrument being studied. If the teacher initiates an atmosphere in which newly acquired information is processed and conclusions are arrived at based on understanding and deduction as opposed to simply being fed facts, the students will find that the subject matter becomes more meaningful and will develop learning skills that are transferable to other information-gathering experiences.

In the spirit of developing higher cognitive skills demanded by the Common Core, the informed approach initiates a learning modality based on the fundamental Common Core principle of deriving information from various related sources. Students broaden their knowledge base by linking certain information/concepts to other related but not apparent information to form new conclusions and, in so doing, acquire new knowledge. This format for learning can then be applied to any topic or learning experience. Constructivism becomes the nucleus of a Common Core approach, integrating learning experiences into a broad-based homogenization of subject matter. Consequently, intellectual independence is achieved.

Understanding how something works makes it easier to work. If one understands that shorter strings produce higher notes, it is possible to determine the fingering for all string instruments through observation, computation, and deduction without the aid of a fingering chart. The same is true of all other instruments. Adjusting the length of the tone-amplifying portion of an instrument through the use of valves or keys alters the pitch. Smaller or shorter is higher, whereas bigger or longer is lower. Through understanding the greater picture, the smaller details become markedly more apparent.

Chapter Four

The Common Core and the Constructivist Approach

By introducing small segments of appropriate supplementary material not usually included in but relevant to an instrumental music lesson, what might be a routine session can become an expanded learning experience. This approach can stimulate the thought process and the deductive reasoning associated with the constructivist learning theory. Material showing how instrument family members relate to each other, their similarities and differences, and how they produce sounds can greatly broaden the scope of a session, bringing it beyond the ordinary. Understanding how something works makes it easier to work it.

The following chapters provide topics and materials that can be used to augment instrumental music lessons. The material gives a broad overview of how the instruments work and provides subject matter that can be used in planning lessons to follow up on the "teach a man to fish" and constructivist philosophy discussed in chapter 3. Each subject is introduced with a "topic justification" explaining its value and is followed by the subject information. Specific lesson plans are not offered because the material is intended to be used at the discretion of the teacher when relevant to the instrument lesson, and as an adjunct to the ongoing instrument-learning experience.

Play First; Talk Later: It is imperative that supplementary material be just that, a supplement to learning to play and actually playing an instrument. Although supplementary material is interesting and relevant to the playing experience, young people are anxious and excited about handling instruments and making sounds. Ergo, "Play first; talk later." The teacher's challenge is to incorporate the very relevant supplementary material into the traditional lesson without its becoming a talk fest in place of a playing experience. A reminder will precede every chapter.

Notes to the teacher justifying the use of the topic at hand appear in italics. This is followed by subject matter in traditional type. Interesting facts about the instruments and how they work are presented under individual headings to aid the reader in finding a particular topic.

An example of how to use this material to enhance a lesson might be to include a brief discussion on the structural and sound-producing similarities of the different instruments in an instrument family being studied.

- For string instruments, a point of interest could be how the combined tuning of the strings of a violin, viola, cello and double bass overlap, generally parallel to the range of the four human voices, and provide the string section of an orchestra with playing range that allows it to be the leading force in a symphony orchestra.
- For brass instruments, the function of the valve as a device used to extend the length of the tubing to lower the open tones is an excellent topic that will bring awareness to the process of learning fingering by deduction rather than instruction.
- For woodwind instruments, demonstrate the same principles of longer instruments making lower sounds as the open tone holes on each instrument are closed in descending order from the top down.
- For percussion instruments, explain how the category is vast and includes instruments of indefinite and definite pitch along with every possible item that can make a sound by being struck, rubbed, shaken, or blown into. Because the percussion instrument category is so broad, it is represented in all four of the general categories of musical instruments.

Introducing students to this global concept of musical-instrument categorization can significantly widen their horizons.

Instrument Classifications: The four broad categories of musical instruments are idiophones, chordophones, aerophones, and membranophones. These terms are used for all acoustic musical instruments. There are percussion instruments in each category. A useful expansion of this exercise would be to ask students whether they can name other instruments in each category.

- *Idiophones* are instruments that, when activated, produce sound through the vibration of the entire instrument. An example would be cymbals, bells, and chimes. When struck, these instruments respond with their entire structure to produce sound. Idiophones can be made of almost any material that can vibrate.
- *Chordophones* are instruments having strings that produce their sounds. In order for a chordophone to be in the percussion family, the strings on the instrument must produce sound by being struck with a mallet or other

hammer-like item. A hammered dulcimer and a piano are examples of chordophones.

- *Aerophones* are instruments that produce sound by a flow of air from any source. In the percussion family, whistles and sirens fall into that category.
- *Membranophones* are instruments that contain some form of membrane as part of their structure and produce sound when that membrane is struck or agitated in some way. Drums are membranophones since they are constructed with a membrane stretched over a shell.

An additional unofficial category of percussion instruments is a catchall to cover the countless items that are not necessarily musical instruments and can produce sound by any of the means described above and that are used in some manner in music performance. These fall into any of the four above-mentioned official categories, but with somewhat dubious justification for being called musical instruments. Included would be anvils, pots and pans, car horns, and almost anything that will make a sound when agitated in any manner. The use of percussion instruments of this nature is most commonly found in twentieth-century or popular music. It is this catchall category that results in percussion instruments being the largest category of instruments in the field.

Chapter Five

Supplementary String Lesson Material

Reminder: "Play first; talk later." *This chapter is devoted to supplementary material for lessons on nonfretted string instruments. The topics are all important additions to the well-informed musical mind; however, supplementary material should never dominate a lesson intended to have students actually play an instrument.*

Construction: *A worthwhile addition to a string-instrument lesson would be identifying the parts of the instrument and how those parts interact with each other.*

The Structure: (The violin will be used as a model for all the instruments in the string family). Figure 5.1 is a diagram of the violin, naming the exterior parts. The mechanism that supports the strings consists of the scroll (A), peg box (B), pegs (C), neck (D), fingerboard (E), bridge (F), saddle (G), tailpiece (H), tailgut (I), and end button (J). The body of the instrument is made up of a top (belly) (K), "f" holes (L), sides (ribs or bouts) (M), a back (back plate) (N), and purfling (O) surrounding the top and back plates. These parts form the exterior of the body.

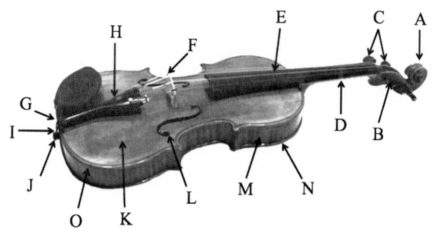

Figure 5.1.

Inside the instrument (figure 5.2), supporting the exterior, are the ribs (A), top and bottom block (B), corner blocks (C), bass bar (D), and soundpost (E).

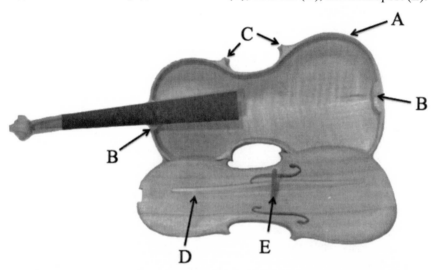

Figure 5.2.

The violin and viola share all the parts described above. The cello differs in that it does not have a chin rest for obvious reasons and has an end pin in place of the violin's end button.

The double bass also has an adjustable end pin. The other significant difference is found in the worm and gear machine head tuning device, which is almost exclusive to the double bass because of the thickness of the strings.

Materials: The materials most commonly used for the construction of these instruments are spruce, maple, ebony, and rosewood. The tops are generally made of spruce since it is a softer wood and fills the design requirements for the most effective sound amplification. Spruce is also used for the soundpost, linings, and the bass bar.

The back, sides, neck, and scroll are made of hard maple, again in compliance with the need to achieve the most responsive amplifier while maintaining structural integrity. Hard maple or a wood of similar strength is needed for these parts to support the tension exerted by the tuned strings stretched across the instrument.

The trim on the instruments—namely, the end button, saddle, tailpiece, fingerboard, nut, and pegs—is usually made of ebony, rosewood, or, in the case of lower-quality instruments, less expensive hardwoods, metal, or plastic.

All of these instruments are constructed of the same materials and essentially use the same technology in practically the same manner. The only difference will be found in the size and proportions of the larger instruments. In the construction of less-expensive larger instruments, laminated wood is used to cut costs while improving the instrument's structural integrity.

The Instrument Back: There are two ways that wood can be cut for use to make the upper and lower plates (top and back) of an instrument. If it is the intention of the maker to construct an instrument with a two-piece back plate, the wood is cut into a triangular-shaped block that is then cut vertically down the middle to form two triangles. These are then joined to form one plate that is subsequently carved into shape. This process is used in order to increase the likelihood of achieving a symmetrical wood-grain pattern.

The second possibility is to cut a layer of wood to produce a one-piece plate, eliminating the middle seam. The disadvantage of this method is the likelihood that because of the size of span required, a one-piece slab of wood will have a variation in grain as the cut progresses. It is more desirable to maintain a uniform grain in these plates for aesthetic and acoustic reasons. The triangle cut maintains this uniformity because the cuts are taken from a smaller portion of the overall slab of wood.

The Sound Trip: *A knowledge of how instruments work significantly facilitates learning how to play them.*

The violin, viola, cello, and double bass are very similar in their design, acoustics, and construction as well as in their playing techniques and fingering patterns. When a string is set into motion, its vibration is conducted by the bridge to the top of the instrument, transferred via the soundpost to the instrument's back, and distributed laterally throughout the top by the bass bar. The top and back of an instrument are supported by its sides. The combined motion of these parts sets the air contained within the body into a pumping motion that forces the resonating sound out of the instrument through the f holes. The purfling controls the vibration of sound throughout the top and back while reinforcing the structure of those two parts of the instrument.

The Open Strings: *Understanding the relationship of an instrument to other instruments in the same family eases the transition from solo to ensemble playing. Comparing the pitches to which the strings of the four instruments of the family are tuned provides an insight into how these instruments are able to complement one another in ensemble playing. Point out how each instrument in descending order takes on the strings of its upper cousin and then continues on a descending path to eventually encompass most of the musical range.*

The strings on a violin, viola, and cello are tuned in fifths. The double bass is tuned in fourths. Starting from the lowest string, the instruments are tuned as follows:

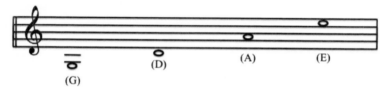

Figure 5.3.

Figure 5.4.

Figure 5.5.

Figure 5.6.

Fingering: *A concept that has anecdotally proven to be successful in accelerating learning to play an instrument deals with how fingering is taught. Don't introduce one note at a time. Students who understand the* *entire process by which an instrument produces different notes will be equipped to determine fingerings without the need for a fingering chart. That ability develops self-confidence, which is one of the byproducts of an in-depth understanding of a subject. "If you know how it works, it is easier to work it."*

The fingering patterns for the violin, viola, and cello are very similar. The player is able to raise the pitch of each string in half steps or in any interval up to seven steps above the open string by depressing the string to the fingerboard in the correct place with the fingers of the left hand.

Positions: Understanding the relationship of fingering positions on the instruments and noting the similarities will help players transition from one instrument to another.

The term *position* refers to the placement of a player's first finger on an instrument's fingerboard in relation to the open string.

When the first finger is placed a half step above an open string, it is called half position; whole step, first position; one and a half steps, second position; two and a half steps, third position; three and a half steps, fourth position; four steps, fifth position; five steps, sixth position; and six steps, seventh position.

Intervals: The fingering patterns for the violin and viola are the same except for the spacing between the fingers, which is slightly larger on the viola. On both instruments, the distance between each finger can be adjusted to produce intervals of either a half step or a whole step. Adding fingers adds steps. Adding multiple fingers produces intervals.

Fingering for the cello follows the same pattern except that there is a half position for every full position. The pattern is as follows: 1/2, 1st, 2nd, 2 1/2, 3rd, 3 1/2, 4th, 5th, 5 1/2, 6th, 6 1/2, and 7th. Each of these positions progresses by half steps up to the seventh position. Note that although violinist and violist can play five half steps in each position, the cellist can play only three half steps. There are no half positions for the first and fourth positions because of the natural half step between E and F and B and C.

Fingering for the double bass follows a slightly different pattern since its larger size requires a greater spread between notes and because the ring finger is not used alone but in conjunction with the pinky. Used individually, the ring finger and pinky both lack strength. The pattern for the positions on the double bass, starting from an open string, is: 1/2, 1st, 2nd, 2 1/2, 3rd, 3 1/2, 4th, 5th, 5 1/2, 6th, 6 1/2, 7th. Each of these positions progresses by half steps up to the seventh position. Note that the double bass player is restricted to playing only three half steps in a position because the third and fourth fingers are used in combination. As with the cello, there are no half positions on the double bass for the first and fourth positions because of the natural half step between E and F and B and C in the diatonic scale.

Comparing the Siblings: *A well-informed musician should possess knowledge beyond that of the player's primary instrument. The four instruments of the violin family are often mistaken for being just increasingly larger versions of the violin. There is more to it than that. The degree to which a teacher should pursue this topic should be commensurate with the grade level and performance level of the class.*

The Violin: The violin is the most acoustically perfect of the four instruments of the family. The viola, cello, and double bass are progressively (but not proportionately) larger while still maintaining essentially the same structure and design as the violin. However, their acoustical perfection does wane as their sizes increase.

The Viola: The viola is often mistakenly described as being a large violin because both instruments share many characteristics of design, physics, construction, and appearance. The viola is tuned a fifth lower than the violin but is one-seventh larger, making the difference in pitch disproportionate to the difference in size. This ratio of tuning to size results in the darker timbre associated with the viola. While the body of a full-size violin is almost always the same size, fourteen inches (35.5 cm) long, the size of a viola body can vary as much as four inches. What are considered full-size viola bodies can range from thirteen and a half inches to eighteen inches in length with the widths and depths ranging proportionate to the increased length.

Another difference between the violin and viola is found in the size-to-pitch ratio. An instrument that is tuned a perfect fifth below the violin should be considerably larger than the viola if it were to follow the size-to-pitch ratio set by the design of the violin. In fact, the size of the viola should be so great that playing it under the chin would not be manageable. Since the viola is not correctly proportioned to its tuning, viola makers can enjoy a bit of latitude when designing the instrument and can alter the size to produce the tone quality desired.

The Cello: The cello, or violoncello, is also disproportionate in size to its difference in tuning. It is tuned a full octave below the viola but is smaller than its acoustical requirement. The discrepancy is compensated for by a significant increase in the depth or thickness of the body of the instrument. Because of the increased depth, the lower tones are able to resonate with the characteristic cello timbre. Because of its relatively large size, the cello is supported by an end pin that extends from the bottom of the instrument and is adjustable to accommodate players of various sizes.

Because the cello in the playing position rests on the floor, the strings are the reverse from those found on the violin and viola. In playing position the lowest string, the C string becomes the first string on the player's right hand, as opposed to violins and violas, which in playing position have the highest string at the player's right side.

The Double Bass: The double bass is the lowest-sounding instrument of the string family. Although it also shares many of the features of the other string instruments, the double bass has the greatest structural differences of the family. Unlike the violin and viola pegs, double bass pegs do not function on the wooden wedge principle. Because of the greater thickness of double bass strings, there is need for a stronger and more stable peg. This necessity produced the worm-and-gear system now used on all double basses.

The worm-and-gear system is used on fretted string instruments and can be installed on any of the other three instruments of the violin family. Such a modification is usually restricted to use on student instruments to help facilitate tuning. Unfortunately, the mechanism adds a considerable amount of weight to the pegbox and, consequently, the advantages of easier tuning are outweighed by a possible problem of balance on the violin or viola. The use of the worm-and-gear system is more practical on the cello and the double bass since these instruments rest on the floor, and balance is less of a burden to the player.

At this writing there are several new mechanical pegs that the manufacturers claim work on a nonslip gear system. The pegs look like traditional ones, need to be installed by a luthier, cost about $100 per set, and have not yet developed a track record.

In addition to its larger size, the double bass differs slightly in shape from the violin, viola, and cello. While the shoulders of these instruments are at a 90-degree angle from the fingerboard, the size of the double bass requires that the shoulders be sloped in order to allow the player to comfortably reach over them to the higher playing positions.

Another difference is found in the back of some double basses. Rather than always being rounded, the back of the larger instruments starts out from the heel of the neck, slopes outward, and then levels off to a flat back for the major portion of the instrument. This design allows the maker to use less than half the wood required for a rounded back without sacrificing any structural integrity.

Some double basses have a fifth string, enabling the performer to play down to C, a third below the low E string on the instrument. An additional way to achieve this extended range is by installing a device that lowers the pitch of the fourth string to C.

Strings: *A knowledge of how string construction affects the sound of an instrument is essential for any serious string player. The topic is seldom addressed in a string-instrument class, yet strings are the nucleus of the sound-production mechanism of these instruments.*

Among the most common materials used to make strings are gut, steel, perlon (a type of stranded plastic fiber), nylon, silk, chromium/steel, and gold. With the exception of the gold strings, all the other products can be used as a core for strings that are then wrapped with aluminum, chromium, or silver.

At this point a wound string can be unraveled to demonstrate its construction.

The winding process can be used for all strings except the violin E string, which, because of its high pitch, does not require the acoustical enhancement provided by winding.

Each type of string construction and combination of materials produce a different sound, so it is possible to alter the overall tone quality of an instrument by just changing the strings. One can brighten or darken the tone quality of an instrument or alter the tone projection or amplitude by selecting string material that will produce the desired effect. The teacher may have on hand two strings of the same category. An example would be cello D strings, each made of entirely different materials, such as a gut core with aluminum winding or perlon core with silver winding. Install them both on the same instrument side by side, one in the D position and the other in the G position. Tune them both to D and listen to the difference.

Steel core strings are most durable, produce the most aggressive, brightest sound, stay in tune longer, and are generally prescribed for use by beginning players. Because of steel's strength, the strings can be made with less material, thereby increasing the production of upper partials in a given pitch while improving bowing response.

Gut strings are made of the entrails of animals. These strings produce a more mellow sound, but since they react to changes in temperature and humidity, they are highly susceptible to pitch problems and tend to break more easily. Gut core strings, which are wound with silver or aluminum, retain the characteristics of pure gut but tend to have a fuller sound and somewhat greater durability. It is the winding on the gut core that allows the core to be thinner and, therefore, more responsive.

Synthetic core strings are made with nylon or other manufactured substances. The synthetic core is intended to reproduce the positive attributes of a gut core string, but it is stronger than gut, does not react greatly to temperature and humidity changes, and tends to stay in tune longer. Strings manufactured in this fashion produce a brighter, more robust sound than gut strings.

Demonstrate with examples of how strings are constructed, with either a loop end, ball end, or knot end. A hands-on exercise can be conducted where students install the various types of strings by inserting them in the keyhole-shaped hole of a tailpiece or directly onto a fine tuner. The loop and ball ends are usually found on most strings, whereas the knot end is used for gut strings without windings. The lesson might conclude with the fact that strings are produced in a wide range of thicknesses.

Strings are categorized by some manufacturers as light, medium, or heavy. Others use a proprietary system of numbers to identify their string sizes. When the terms *light*, *medium*, and *heavy* are applied to strings, those labels allege the string to have sound and bowing responses commensurate with their labels. Lighter strings respond easily and allow the player to produce a wider spectrum of more sensitive sounds but with less volume. Heavy-tension strings produce fuller dynamic tone and volume, but they do so at the expense of bowing response and flexibility. Medium-labeled strings strike a balance between the two extremes. There are no industry-wide standards for this nomenclature, so there can be significant variations between similar labels from different manufacturers. A comparison trial of strings of supposedly the same tension from several different manufacturers would be one way to decide on the best string for an individual player.

Bridge: *A bridge transfers sound from a vibrating string to the body (amplifier) of an instrument. A discussion of bridge design, the material used to make one, and its placement and fit on an instrument will help equip the student to maintain a bridge so it will function in the best possible way.*

When a bow is properly drawn across a string, the sound that is generated is conducted to the top or belly of the instrument by the bridge. As the string vibrates, its transverse (side-to-side) motion is converted by the bridge into a perpendicular (up and down) "stamping" motion. The feet of the bridge transfer the vibrations to the belly of the instrument. (See chapter 19 for information on bridge placement on an instrument and how the bridge feet should fit the contour of the instrument's top.)

As strings are tuned, they gradually pull the bridge toward the fingerboard in small, almost-unnoticeable increments. To prevent the bridge from falling or warping, it is necessary to tilt it slightly back toward the tailpiece as needed. The following describes the process of setting the bridge on various string instruments.

The Violin and Viola: This adjustment is achieved for the violin or viola by first loosening the strings slightly and then placing the instrument on one's lap with the fingerboard facing away from the body. Using the thumb and forefinger of each hand, grip the bridge on either side and bend it back to its upright position. The bridge feet should be in perfect contact with the top of the instrument. Retune the instrument.

The Cello: For the cello, loosen the strings slightly. Holding the cello in playing position, lean over the shoulders of the instrument to reach down to the bridge, and with the thumb and forefinger of each hand, grip the bridge on either side and bend it back to its upright position. Retune the cello.

The Double Bass: For the double bass, loosen the strings slightly, lay the instrument on its back on a soft rug surface, and move the bridge to its upright position. Then retune the bass.

For All Instruments: After tuning, make a quick check of the bridge by viewing it from the tailpiece side to be sure that the feet are in total contact with the top of the instrument. When viewing the bridge from its side, the side facing the tailpiece should be at a perfect 90-degree angle from the top of the instrument, whereas the fingerboard side of the bridge will be graduated to a smaller thickness toward its top.

Bridge Dimensions: *This topic would be suitable for a more advanced group and can be presented when incorrect bridge dimensions are causing a problem. Since the bridge plays a dominant role in transferring the sound from the strings to the body of the instrument, the design and material used to make the bridge, how it is cut to fit the instrument, and its placement on the instrument must be calculated to fill its function in the best possible way. (See chapter 19 for more information on the subject.)*

Climate Changes: *Bridge height can sometimes change when the belly or top of an instrument rises or lowers with a change in the temperature and/ or humidity. This topic can best be introduced when the issue actually occurs with an instrument being used. (See chapter 19 for more on this topic.)*

The soundpost and bass bar, both hidden inside the instrument, are the "soul" of a stringed instrument. As such, their existence, location, and function should be part of a player's understanding. The following material can be used in planning a lesson on this topic.

Soundpost: The soundpost plays an important role in sound transmission. In addition to acting as a structural support for the top of the instrument, this post, made of soft wood such as spruce, conducts the vibrations from the top of the instrument to its back. The soundpost distributes tones produced by the higher strings to the back of the instrument while muting any echo effect that would occur if the post were not present.

Bass Bar: The bass bar also serves two functions. Located on the underside of the top of the instrument directly beneath the bridge foot for lower strings, the bass bar reinforces the instrument, supporting the great force exerted by the tension of the strings. It also distributes the vibrations laterally throughout the top.

The soundpost and bass bar together distribute sound throughout the body. This distribution acts as an amplifier for the sounds generated by the strings. The motion of the components stimulates the air pocket contained within the body into vibrating patterns of compression and rarefaction. The sound generated at the string is transported through the bridge, belly, soundpost, and bass bar to ultimately produce the tone of the instrument.

Review of How They Work: *This topic is of a general nature and can be associated with lessons on tone production and timbre as well as instrument adjustments. Understanding how string instruments process sound is fundamental to many of the mechanical and playing activities associated with string instruments.*

The complete amplifying process of violin-family instruments takes place as follows: The string's vibrations are conducted by the hardwood (usually maple) bridge to the softer wood (usually spruce) top plate. The vibrations are then transported via the softwood soundpost to the hardwood back of the instrument and via the softwood bass bar laterally throughout the entire top.

The hardwood back and softer wood top (belly) are joined by hardwood sides. Combined, the top, sides, and back form an air space in which the sound circulates. The interaction of all of these components forms the amplifier for the sound produced by the strings. The combined motion of the parts sets the volume of air contained within the body of the instrument into a pumping motion that forces the resonating sound out of the instrument through the f holes. In this manner the instruments produce sound.

Additional Information: *A few seldom-discussed facts about violin-family instruments might be brief sidelights to inject into a lesson at the appropriate time.*

The Sides and Back: The sides and back of the instrument are usually made of maple. This is a harder wood than spruce, which is used for the belly of the violin. The function of the sides and back, in addition to enhancing the vibrating process, is to form the supporting structure for the entire instrument.

String Tension: The tension incurred by the strings stretched from the top (pegs) to the bottom (tailpiece), some 68 lbs (31 kg) for the violin, draws the top (scroll end) and bottom of the instrument (tailpiece end) toward each other. It is the strength of the back plate combined with the sides that prevents the instrument from folding in half.

F Holes: The f holes significantly affect the tone quality of an instrument. The flexing action of the middle portion of the top and the ability of the tone-saturated air within the sound box to escape are affected by the size, shape, and location of the holes. Because of the importance of these shapely orifices, their exact shape, size, and location are distinct to each craftsperson.

Purfling: The purfling is two parallel strips of hard wood, usually ebony, that are inlaid into the surface around the edge of the top and back of instruments in the violin family. The groove cut into the wood's surface for the inlay acts as a barrier or interruption for the vibration that is traveling through the wood. Using purfling, the instrument maker is able to define clearly the area throughout which the vibration takes place and thereby control that vibrating area and the tone it produces. Purfling also reinforces the edge of the instrument, helping to prevent the wood from chipping.

Instrument Care: *Instrument care should be a part of the curriculum presented on an as-needed basis. The information needed for these lessons for string instruments will be found in chapter 19. The topics listed below are recommended for insertion into regular lessons when appropriate. Reminder: play first; talk later.*

Storage: The fact that string instruments are hygroscopic (they readily take up and retain moisture) and can sustain significant damage when subjected to extreme temperatures and humidity should be explained and then reiterated on a regular basis in an effort to prevent any damage caused by improper storage. When not in use, a string instrument should always be kept in a case and stored in an environment that is comfortable for a human being. For more information, see chapter 19.

Cracks: Should a crack occur or seam open, avoid touching that area since any deposit of skin oils or perspiration can inhibit the effectiveness of the glue used in the repair process. Any such damage should be reported to the teacher immediately.

Teachers should make clear that cracking or open seams are not the student's fault; students should not hesitate to report such damage for fear of being blamed for it.

Traveling: When traveling with an instrument, keep the instrument in the same location you occupy en route.

Cleaning: After each use, wipe the surfaces of the instrument and the strings with a soft cotton cloth to remove any rosin dust, natural skin oils, and perspiration. These will accumulate and, if left to permeate the surface of the instrument, will cause damage that could affect the sound and diminish the instrument's value. Use a separate cloth for the strings and body to avoid spreading rosin dust on the instrument and instrument polish on the strings.

For All String Instruments: After tuning, make a quick check of the bridge to be sure that the feet are in total contact with the top of the instrument (see chapter 19).

Routine Adjustments: *These are adjustments that are ongoing. As string instruments are being played, the parts of the instruments are dynamic and continuously in motion. These movements are minute and not readily visible, but do build up to ultimately become a playing problem and, at worst, can damage the instrument.*

More detailed information on related topics listed below can be found in chapter 19.

Pegs: A reoccurring seasonal problem with violins, violas, and cellos is slipping or sticking pegs. See chapter 19.

Fine Tuner: A fine tuner requires periodic adjustments. See chapter 19.

Strings: Strings are in continuous contact with the nut, bridge, and tail-piece on an instrument. It is, therefore, important to pay periodic attention to those points of contact to ensure that they are wearing properly and are in optimum adjustment to produce the best sound.

Nut: The nut, located directly below the pegbox, controls the distribution of the four strings across the fingerboard as well as the strings' distance or height from the fingerboard. Check the nut periodically for wear caused by the strings at their point of contact. See more information on this topic in chapter 19.

Tailpiece: The final point of contact the strings have is with the tailpiece, which exists in a variety of forms from a simple plastic unit to the most elaborate hand-carved ivory work of art. The size, density of material, and location of the tailpiece in relation to the bridge, along with the tailgut adjustment, are all factors that affect the vibration of the strings. Careful attention must be given to these issues when a tailpiece is being fitted.

Tailpieces are made with either one built-in fine tuner for each string or without any built-in fine tuners. Tailpieces with built-in fine tuners are made of metal or plastic and are very convenient for use on student instruments. Advanced players are usually satisfied with adding only one fine tuner to a tailpiece for the instrument's highest string. Keeping the four-fine-tuner tailpiece is a matter of individual choice.

Saddle: The saddle is a small piece of ebony or other hard wood that is placed at the end of an instrument's body. This hard wood acts as a support for the tail gut, preventing it from damaging the softer spruce wood instrument top. A saddle should be fitted so that there is sufficient space on either side for the inevitable expansion and contraction of the spruce top. If the saddle is too tightly fitted, when that expansion takes place a crack in the top at either side of the saddle could occur. Should this happen, the saddle should be refitted by a luthier and the crack repaired.

Summary: Violins, violas, cellos, and double basses require similar procedures and equipment for proper maintenance. The owner or renter should take the time to develop an understanding of how these instruments react to their environment and to their being handled on a long- term basis. Prepared with that understanding, teachers and students will find that maintaining the instruments will be a matter of establishing simple, routine procedures to be used after each playing session along with other, more elaborate procedures to be carried out by a luthier periodically as needed.

Bows: The bow is the sound generator on a string instrument, a concept that is often given short shrift in string classes. A knowledge of how bows are made, how the hair is installed, and how it interacts with the strings will produce an informed rather than reactive user. Understanding how the bows of the four instruments in the violin family differ will assist in transitioning from one instrument to another in the same family.

Introduction: The phrase "good instrument + bad bow = bad sound" summarizes the issue in the simplest terms. The topics to cover in a lesson are the material from which the stick is made, the kind of hair on it, the balance of the bow, its camber, the stability of the frog, its ease of movement, and, finally, mention of cosmetic adornments, if present. See chapter 19 for more detailed information on this topic.

The Stick: The stick of a bow is its spine. It can be made of any wood or some manmade substances such as carbon fiber or fiberglass.

Note: If possible, have a sample of each kind of stick for the students to examine. A local dealer should be happy to lend the needed bows for this use.

Show the difference among pernambuco, brazilwood, carbon fiber, and fiberglass bow sticks.

Wood: If they are available, place several wooden bows side by side on a table and have the students examine the bows closely, looking for differences and imperfections in the wood grain of each. Then have the students handle and use each bow, playing the same note patterns to see if they are able to detect different responses.

Pernambuco: Describe how pernambuco is the best wood for bow sticks but that it has become scarce because of restrictions set by the Brazilian government due to overharvesting of the tree from which it comes.

Other Choices: Explain how brazilwood, pearwood, and other woods along with fiberglass and carbon fiber are now being used in place of pernambuco but with varying degrees of quality sacrifice. Return to the trial activity used to compare bows made with various materials, and have the students distinguish among them.

Camber: Camber refers to the arch shape of the stick of a well-made bow. Have the students compare the camber of various bows with the bow hair loose. Then tighten the hair to playing firmness and compare the bows again to judge how the various sticks responded to the hair tension. This will most likely illustrate the individuality of each wooden bow stick along with the uniformity of the bow sticks constructed of synthetic products such as fiberglass and carbon fiber.

Flexibility: The flexibility of bow sticks can vary greatly. Round sticks are usually soft and tend to be more yielding to pressure. Consequently, round sticks will result in a generally gentler response. Octagonal sticks are firmer than round sticks and will respond with a crisper, more aggressive sound.

Balance and Weight: A bow's weight and balance are very significant factors in a player's bow control. Awareness of this issue, however, is seldom present in the minds of young players. Even more unfortunate is the lack of attention some teachers give to this issue. A good introduction to the topic might consist of a teacher selecting bows with significantly different weights and balances and having the students play their instrument with these different bows. To exaggerate the issue, have the students play their instruments with bows from instruments that are either larger or smaller than theirs in order to feel the effects of incorrect balance and weight.

The correct weight and balance for a bow is that which is comfortable and responsive for the individual using it. See chapter 14 for some exercises in bow trials.

Horsehair: An interesting but little-discussed fact is that when viewed with the naked eye, horsehair appears to be smooth, but under examination with a microscope, the surface of the hair is quite rough. Particles called follicles project from the hair and form an abrasive surface.

Rosin, a tree sap derivative, is applied to bow hair to increase its gripping power. When rosined, bow hair is drawn across a string on an instrument, and the hair grips the string and excites it into motion, which causes the vibration that produces a tone. As the bow is drawn across a string, the bow hair appears to be in constant contact with the string. However, this is not the case. Instead, what is occurring is the bow hair gripping and releasing the string in a rapid sequence, replicating a plucking action. This action causes the string to be drawn to a point where its lateral tension is sufficient to overcome the gripping force of the rosined bow hair. At that point, the string releases itself from the bow and proceeds to its opposite lateral extreme, only to repeat the process. The final effect is one of a string gripped by the bow hair, pulled to a point of tension, breaking free from that grip, rebounding to a point opposite that from which it was just released, and then being caught again by the bow hair to start the process again. All of this occurs in such rapid succession that it is not visible to the naked eye.

Bow Care: *See chapter 19 for detailed information on this topic.*

Summary: A bow is as important a part of an instrument outfit as is the instrument itself. Bow selection, care, and use, which are often given short shrift, should be part of a well-balanced string-instrument curriculum.

Chapter Six

Supplementary Woodwind Lesson Material

Reminder: "Play first; talk later."

Woodwind Instruments: *Woodwind instruments share many physical and operational characteristics. They also have some differences. Enlightening students to both the similarities and differences will help them handle their own instrument and also transition from one instrument to another should they want to double.*

Because the following information is a bit abstract, an actual woodwind instrument should be used as part of the lesson to illustrate and demonstrate every step. The students can then follow up with experimentation on their own instrument.

How They Work: *Understanding how a woodwind instrument converts the squawk that is emitted from a reed or the toot from a flute's embouchure hole into desirable music tones facilitates learning and reinforces confidence. Remember the leitmotif, "If you know how it works, it is easier to work it."*

What Happens Inside the Instrument: Woodwind instruments have three basic operating systems: sound generating, sound amplification, and a sound-manipulating key system.

Sound Generation: Some woodwind instruments produce sound through a single reed held on to a mouthpiece with a ligature as on a clarinet or saxophone, or a double reed as on an oboe, English horn, or bassoon. Others use a flat, shelf-like surface positioned to allow a stream of air to undulate over and under the edge of the shelf, as on a flute or recorder.

Amplification: The body of a woodwind instrument is the sound amplifier. The sound generator coupled with the body is limited to producing only those sounds that are fundamental to the instrument. The sound generator will stimulate the column of air inside the body to vibrate. That vibrating column is only as long as the distance from the sound generator to the first open hole on the body. The sound being produced will be the frequency that results from the length of that vibrating column.

Other Sounds: To lower the pitch of the basic sound, it is necessary to extend the length of the vibrating column—thus the need for a key system. These systems, added to the basic design of the instrument's body, permit the player to lengthen or shorten the vibrating column of air in small increments. By so doing, the player can produce the pitches that lie between the fundamentals on wind instruments. As the vibrating column of air is shortened, the pitch is raised. Conversely, as the vibrating column of air is lengthened, the pitch is lowered.

Observation: Bigger or longer instruments produce lower sounds; conversely, smaller or shorter instruments produce higher sounds.

Why We Need Keys: The laws of physics dictate the location and size of the tone holes on the body of a woodwind instrument. Unfortunately, the requirements set by these laws do not coincide with the structure of the human hand, so to fulfill the need for more notes and greater versatility, mechanical means had to be found to extend the potential span of the fingers. Thus began the introduction of keys on woodwind instruments. Using the modern key system, it is possible to control the opening and closing of tone holes regardless of their location on the body of an instrument.

Keys: *Key systems for all woodwind instruments use the same principles of leverage and are described by the same terminology. The following tells about different kinds of keys and some facts about them.*

Open- and Closed-Key Terminology: There are two basic types of keys, open and closed. The term *open key*, when used in the broadest sense, refers to a key that, at rest, is not covering the hole it serves. When the key is at rest, that hole is open, but it has a key to cover it when necessary. The term *closed key*, when used in its broadest sense, refers to a key that, at rest, covers and seals the hole it serves. Both types of keys, when activated, produce the inverse effect that their names imply, that is, when activated, a closed key opens the hole it covers, whereas an open key closes the hole it covers.

The terms *open* and *closed* are not to be confused with similar terms used to describe the open-hole, French, or perforated keys, or closed-hole, plateau keys of the flute. The flute open-hole keys actually have a hole in the middle of the key. The flute closed-hole or plateau key is as the name implies. It has no hole in it. Most musicians believe that open-hole (French) keys produce a better sound than the closed-hole (plateau) keys since the open design strengthens the upper partials of each note, thereby enriching the sound.

Key Construction: Keys of modern design follow basic principles of leverage using a fulcrum as a pivot point on which the key rocks when activated. There are three parts to a key mechanism. The part in contact with the player's finger is called either the paddle, the spatula, or the finger. On the opposite end of the key is the pad cup, which contains a pad, most often made of felt, covered with leather, fish skin, or sheep skin. When the key is closed, the pad covers the tone hole. The paddle and cup are joined by a stem called an arm, which in turn is connected to a hollow tube called a hinge tube, on which the key rocks back and forth.

Key Springs: The three types of springs used to provide the tension required to return a key to its position of rest are wire springs, needle springs, and flat springs. A wire spring is a strip of wire usually made of an alloy cut to the length required by its position on the instrument and inserted into a hole in the post that holds the flute key in place.

Needle springs are needle-shaped, usually made of blue steel, pointed on one end, and flattened on the other end, which are inserted into the instrument's post. Needle springs are much stronger than wire springs and are used on larger instruments like the saxophone.

Flat springs are also made of various metal alloys and are shaped and sized to fit their position on the instrument. A flat spring has a hole drilled in the contact end where a screw is inserted to hold the spring on the key.

Tone-Hole Construction: Tone holes on flutes and saxophones extend out from the body, whereas on other woodwind instruments, tone holes are usually drilled into the instrument's body. Flute and saxophone tone holes can be constructed independently of the body and then soldered in place or drawn from the material of the body itself.

Have students examine their instruments and try to determine which method was used to create their tone holes.

The process used to construct drawn tone holes consists of drilling a small hole in the body of the instrument and then pulling a series of balls of increasingly larger size through the hole. The drawing process pulls the material from inside the body upward, forming a cuplike projection that extends from the instrument's body. The resulting projection is then leveled and its edge is rolled, providing a smooth surface on which the pad can rest. This process creates a smooth extrusion that is thought by some to produce less resistance to the airflow and, therefore, a better tone.

Intonation/Tuning: *Correct intonation is essential to music performance. The source of intonation problems stems from either the player or the instrument. Every instrument has some notes that are inherently out of tune. Those can be dealt with to some degree using various long-established procedures. Poor intonation resulting from the player's embouchure or mouthpiece setup can also be resolved. The first step in improving intonation is to understand the cause. Before attempting to tune an instrument, play it for a minute or two to warm it up.*

General Principles: There is more to playing any instrument in tune than just making a structural adjustment. The overall pitch of an instrument can be changed by adjusting its length. However, when tuning by using this process, not all notes adjust proportionately. Some become in tune while others then become out of tune. Wind instruments depend on the player to produce the sound through his or her embouchure and mouthpiece setup. The degree to which the player learns to control these two factors will ultimately have the most profound effect on intonation. When one starts with a good reed and mouthpiece, playing in tune then becomes a matter of embouchure. Tighter or looser embouchures with proper placement of the mouthpiece in the mouth or on the lips are the factors that control pitch.

Flute: Basic tuning of a flute is achieved by adjusting the crown assembly in the head joint. The crown assembly consists of a screw on which there is a metal plate, followed by a cork that is followed by a second metal plate. Turning this screw will move the assembly in or out of the head joint to tune the instrument.

The cleaning rod that comes with a flute has a mark near the end that serves as a guide for tuning. Place that cleaning rod in the head joint so the mark on the rod is visible through the embouchure hole. Adjust the cork assembly in or out so the cleaning rod mark is in the center of the embouchure hole. The instrument should be in tune. This adjustment is for general tuning.

For a finer adjustment, one can adjust the crown assembly inward to sharpen all notes. However, the lower register will be slightly sharper than its upper octave. Conversely, adjusting the assembly outward will lower all notes, but the higher register will be lowered more than the lower register.

Strive to find the best balance and follow up with moving the head joint slightly inward to raise the pitch or outward to lower it.

Clarinet: When tuning a clarinet, the most commonly used method is to adjust the barrel in or out of the upper joint. To raise the pitch, gently twist the barrel into the upper joint. To lower the pitch, use the same twisting motion to move the barrel out of the upper joint. This method is effective for general tuning; however, not all notes on the instrument respond to that process. If necessary, a more comprehensive tuning can be achieved by using the in and out process on the middle joint of the instrument.

Saxophone: On a saxophone, one can raise or lower the pitch by using a twisting motion to move the mouthpiece slightly in or out of the neck. Moving it inward will raise the pitch, and moving it outward will lower the pitch. Mechanically speaking, this is about all one can do to tune a saxophone. However, as stated earlier, there is more to playing any instrument in tune than just making a structural adjustment.

Oboe: Since the double reed is the mouthpiece on an oboe, one might assume that tuning would be a simple matter of sliding the reed in to raise the pitch and out to lower the pitch. However, when one pulls out the reed to lower the pitch, a space opens between the bottom of the reed, (the staple), and the bore of the instrument. This space interrupts the integrity of the reed/ bore relationship, creating turbulence in the sound producing a vibrating column of air and in so doing affects the tone quality and pitch. Those who are concerned about that issue prefer adjusting intonation via the embou-chure/reed relationship. Adjusting one's embouchure pressure and muscle position can alter the pitch up or down.

An A-440 is usually the note of choice for tuning the oboe. When played by the oboe, the note is traditionally used as the tuning guide for an orchestra. There is no scientific reason for this except to say that the oboe sound is clear, penetrating, and easy to hear above the cacophony of a tuning orches-tra.

Bassoon: The bassoon is a relatively inflexible instrument and therefore difficult to tune. The lower register is all but set by the manufacturer. Adjust-ing the bocal (the curved, tapered tube that connects the body and the reed) will have little effect on the general intonation. True tuning of a bassoon remains a product of the quality of the bocal, reed, the embouchure of the player, and his or her ability to finesse the pitch of the various notes.

Fingering, General Principles: *In the early stages of instruction it is unlikely that a student will have any significant awareness of the other in-struments in the ensemble. Learning that all woodwind instruments are fun-damentally the same facilitates transitioning from one instrument to another, creates a subliminal camaraderie that will enrich the playing experience, and improves ensemble participation with the concept that all woodwind family members share a common bond.*

The fingerings for woodwind instruments are similar for many notes. The flute, oboe, and saxophone are very close, and the clarinet and bassoon also share some similar patterns. With the exception of the saxophone, which does not have a thumb hole, covering the thumb hole and then covering the six open holes one at a time in descending order from the top down will produce a descending series of notes. Depressing the register key with the thumb hole covered will raise all notes on a clarinet a twelfth. On other woodwind instruments, the thumb key will raise the notes an octave. Press-ing the side keys will alter the tones produced when any or all of the six open holes are covered.

Summary: Woodwind instruments are the most mechanically complex of all orchestral instruments. Their complex key systems require greater han-dling care by the player and more frequent attention by a technician. Assem-bly is always an opportunity to dislodge a key or alter an adjustment if the person doing the assembling is not aware of potential pitfalls. This topic should be prominent in the first lesson and repeated in subsequent lessons until it has been securely instilled in the students' minds.

Chapter Seven

Supplementary Brass Lesson Material

Reminder: "Play first; talk later." *The following topics are all very important additions to the well-informed musical mind; however, supplementary material should never dominate a lesson in which it is intended that students actually play an instrument.*

Brass Instruments: *Brass instruments have many common attributes that make doubling and tripling on these instruments relatively easy. An interesting lesson can consist of having students with some degree of facility on their instrument try a closely related instrument of interest. There is significant value in having all brass players understand the general principles of fingering and how they work. In keeping with the adage that "if you know how it work, it is easier to work it," knowledge becomes power.*

Sound Production: *All brass instruments generate sound by the player's lips buzzing into a cup-shaped mouthpiece, part of a very first lesson. The approach generally accepted by brass teachers consists of introducing a basic embouchure position in conjunction with some breathing instruction. It is often necessary to modify the basic embouchure to accommodate physical individualities. Therein lies the teacher's challenge. The basic embouchure position is described below. Any modification must then emanate from the teacher's knowledge, experience, and individual point of view in conjunction with the student's needs.*

Producing Sound: The most commonly accepted instructions used to begin producing a sound on a brass instrument consist of buzzing moistened lips into a cup-shaped mouthpiece with the upper lip producing the primary buzz. Depending on the lip formation of the player, the lower lip generally buzzes to a lesser degree. The lower lip also provides support, acts as a stabilizer for the vibration of the lips, and controls the size of the opening through which the air passes into the mouthpiece.

Experts agree that placement of the mouthpiece on the lips is unique to each embouchure and must ultimately be determined by the player's physical needs. To start, it is recommended that the mouthpiece be placed in the center of the lips with equal amounts of the upper and lower lip in contact with the mouthpiece cup. It is then a matter of adjusting the mouthpiece placement up or down until the position that produces the best sound for that individual is determined.

The pitches produced can be changed by increasing or decreasing the intensity of the buzz. This is accomplished by raising or lowering the corners of the mouth. Pulling the corners of the mouth down will raise the pitch, and raising the corners of the mouth will lower the pitch.

Principles of Fingering: Brass instruments are similar in their acoustical and structural designs. A player can produce a series of open tones without the use of valves. Valves can then be used individually or in combination to lower open tones and produce other tones. When a valve is depressed, the holes in the valve are aligned with an additional length of tubing that is part of the instrument. Longer tubing on an instrument produces lower pitches.

There are two types of valves. The *piston valve* is used on most brass instruments. The *rotary valve* is always used on the French horn and less frequently on other instruments. Although they differ mechanically, using them has the same result. Depressing a valve opens a section of tubing, increasing the length of the instrument and lowering the open tone.

Fingering Patterns: The trumpet will be used as an example for all valve instruments.

Trumpets produce the following open tones with no valves depressed.

Figure 7.1.

By depressing valves, the open tones can be lowered in half-step increments to produce the tones that exist between each open tone.

To lower an open tone one half step, a minor second, depress valve 2.

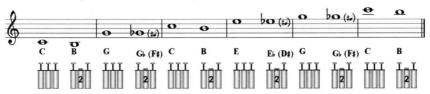

Figure 7.2.

To lower an open tone two half steps, a major second, depress valve 1.

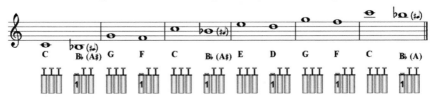

Figure 7.3.

To lower an open tone three half steps, a minor third, depress valve 3 or valves 1 and 2. Note: For better intonation, the preferred fingering for these notes is 1 and 2.

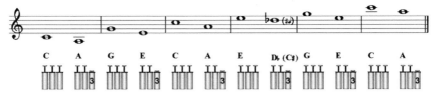

Figure 7.4.

To lower an open tone four half steps, a major third, depress valves 2 and 3.

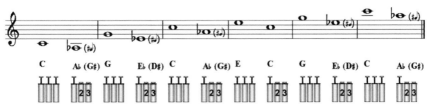

Figure 7.5.

To lower an open tone five half steps, a perfect fourth, depress valves 1 and 3.

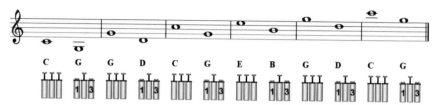

Figure 7.6.

To lower an open tone six half steps, augmented fourth or diminished fifth, depress valves 1, 2, and 3.

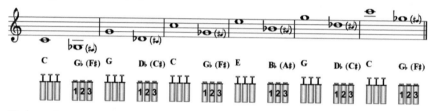

Figure 7.7.

Review: The valves on any brass instrument can be used individually or in combination, lowering an open tone to produce all the other tones that exist below the open tones. The pattern is as follows:

- valve 1 = whole step or a second
- valve 2 = half step or minor second
- valve 3 = step and a half or minor third
- valves 1 + 2 = step and a half or a minor third
- valves 2 + 3 = two whole steps or a major third
- valves 1 + 3 + two and a half steps or a perfect fourth
- valves 1 + 2 + 3 = three whole steps of a diminished fourth

To determine the fingering without a fingering chart for any valve instrument, locate the open tones and apply the above principles.

Tuning: *Because all brass instruments with the exception of the slide trombone have inherent intonation problems, it is impossible to achieve tuning perfection. The challenge for the teacher will be to first provide the instruction needed for the student to play the fundamental tones in tune. From that point, dealing with the individual instrument's pitch anomalies becomes a matter of addressing each one where it is relevant to the activity at hand. Dwelling on one intonation problem that is abstract can quickly wear thin and become a turnoff for a young student.*

The Process: Tuning a brass instrument is achieved by moving slides in or out. The main tuning slide is used to adjust the instrument's basic pitch. Additional slides are used to tune the notes related to the use of each valve.

Extending a slide will lower the pitch. Drawing a slide in will raise the pitch. Among the conditions other than embouchure that can cause pitch problems are playing in extreme ranges (both low and high) and extreme volumes (both loud and soft). Outdoor playing in extreme temperatures will alter the fundamental pitch of an instrument, with cold weather lowering pitch, and hot weather raising it. Using different mutes will alter pitch, as will different-size mouthpiece cups. All of these circumstances can usually be dealt with to a reasonable degree by adjusting conditions.

Intonation Problems: *The inherent intonation problems found in brass instruments cannot be easily compensated for. In the case of beginner or young players, dealing with these situations should be attempted on an as-needed basis. Making students aware of such problems is sound pedagogy. Dwelling on the problems and solutions might prove disheartening, as some intonation issues are often difficult if not almost impossible to correct.*

Overtone Series (Open Tones) Intonation Problems: The overtone series, the open tones on brass instruments, have some inconsistencies in intonation. Tones 1, 2, 4, and 8 are in tune. Tones 5 and 7 are flat. Tones 3 and 6 are sharp. When two tones share the same problem, the lower of the two will be the greater offender. Tone 6 is sharper than tone 3, and tone 7 is flatter than tone 5.

Some intonation problems exist as a result of valve architecture. When combining the first and second, first and third, and all three valves, the notes will be sharp. Using the third valve, or the second and third combined, will produce flat notes.

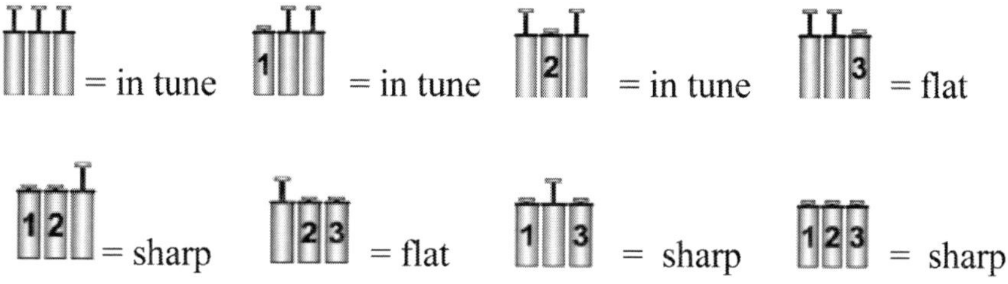

Figure 7.8.

Certain brass instruments such as the euphonium and BB-flat tuba are structured with an auxiliary set of tubing that is used to compensate for the natural rise in pitch inherent in the low register of these instruments. By depressing a fourth valve, additional tubing is opened to lower the pitch for certain notes. This mechanism does not affect the other registers on the instrument.

Summary: Brass instruments are a gift of similarity in their architecture. They all share an embouchure and system of valves and slides that do much the same thing. A brass player can switch from one member of the family to another with relative ease by adjusting to size and fingering patterns. A trumpet player can pick up a tuba and play it within a short time. This is not so with a flute player and a bassoon.

Chapter Eight

Supplementary Percussion Lesson Material

The ability to perform as a percussionist is rooted in understanding and executing the Percussive Arts Society's Forty Essential Snare Drum Rudiments. The level of achievement in this undertaking is the determinant to successfully playing any of the stick or mallet percussion instruments. Fortunately, the Internet abounds with free printed material on all the forty rudiments along with YouTube examples. Many are performed by excellent percussionists.

The website for the Vic Firth Percussion Accessories manufacturer is www.vicfirth.com/education/rudiments.php. On this site, the forty rudiments are presented in detail with performed examples of each. I recommend that all percussion teachers take advantage of the wealth of percussion teaching material presented on the Internet in a manner that could not possibly be matched in print.

In addition to the above, there are a number of topics that should be addressed as sidebars to regularly scheduled lessons. An introduction to the structure of the snare drum and how that architecture relates to all the other drums is important if a student is to learn to properly care for his/her instrument.

In-depth information on the topics to follow can be found in chapters 17 and 22.

Drum Construction: Chapter 22 describes how all drums consist of a shell, one or two heads, and various other parts, depending on the kind of drum. The shell is the body of a drum and the primary support system, while the remaining parts attached to the shell are actively involved in producing sound.

Percussion Care: Learning how to care for one's instrument can be briefly but frequently addressed at appropriate times during a lesson. Talk about how drum heads are made of animal hide or some form of polyester. Explain that while hide is sensitive to changes in ambient temperature and humidity, the polyester heads are much less so. More information on this issue can be found in chapter 22.

The Other Instruments: Introducing students in a percussion session to the instruments they do not play can be a valuable experience. One can tend to live in a world where the only instrument that is important is "the one I play." A snare drummer who knows something about the bass drum, timpani, cymbals, and other instruments that are part of the ensemble is more likely to develop a sense of camaraderie with other percussionists that can lead to increased ensemble cohesiveness and a more unified, better-balanced final musical product.

Bass Drum: Bass drums are similar in structure to snare drums except that bass drums are bigger and have no snare. The three types of bass drums are designed, respectively, for concert use, marching, and dance band or trap sets. More details on this are found in chapter 17.

Timpani: Timpani are definite-pitched (tuned) instruments. They come in a variety of sizes to accommodate the variety of pitches they must produce. Timpani are tuned with tension rods but also have a pedal that is used to quickly change pitches during a performance. See more on this in chapters 17 and 22.

Drum Set: A set of drums consists of a snare drum, bass drum, and floor tom tom, a ride cymbal, crash cymbal, and a hi-hat cymbal. The drum set is used for dance band and small-ensemble playing. Another name for this setup is a trap set. See chapter 17.

Adjusting and tuning drums can make an excellent lesson for a percussion group.

Tuning: Seldom addressed in percussion lessons is the fact that instruments of indefinite pitch such as snare and bass drums can and should be tuned. The tuning procedure, which is essentially the same for all drums, consists of adjusting the tension of the heads to change the sound of the instrument as well as changing the stick rebound. See chapter 22 for complete information on this process.

Electronic Drums: Electronic drums consist of pads with resilient drumhead-like surfaces and a sensor that, when struck, sends an electric impulse through a cable or MIDI connection to a sound-producing and sound-amplifying system. These instruments are versatile, highly portable, and excellent for practice at home, since the volume can be controlled and the instruments are often reasonably priced. Additional information on these products can be found in chapter 17.

Chapter Nine

Meet the Instruments

The first step in developing a new instrumental music program is to establish a recruitment plan. Most young potential students have a limited knowledge of the variety of instruments. Introducing students to the instruments they will have an opportunity to study is an important part of the instrument-selection process. This is the stepping-off point for the direction the students will take in their music future. Although some will change to another instrument, most will remain with their original choice. It is therefore imperative that the teacher make every effort to introduce the students to as many different instruments as possible and to do so using the most effective methods. Determining how to approach this process is dependent on the availability of technology in the school, the instrument inventory the music department enjoys, the ability of the teachers to perform on the instruments, and the geographic location of the school.

Live performances are an excellent medium for developing interest in an instrument. To actually see and hear an instrument played well can be the elixir that can enchant anyone who is predisposed to musical-instrument study to undertake that challenge. A school that is located in or near any major metropolis has access to many of the greatest performers in the world. The extent to which the teacher takes advantage of such cultural treasures is dependent on his or her motivation to identify and contact those individuals.

Renowned performers are often reluctant to get involved in such an undertaking; however, if you don't ask, they won't come. It is not outside the realm of possibility that one will succeed in soliciting the help of a famous performer to take on the task of introducing an instrument to a group of young people. As an alternative to a command performance, the teacher might arrange to have the students take a field trip to a local performance that is appropriate for young students where they can witness the instruments in action.

A more practical approach would be to solicit local working musicians who are interested in promoting their instruments by giving a demonstration. Ads in the print media along with the Internet and the local musicians union abound with names of very competent performers who may be willing to contribute their time to your recruitment process. The more local they are, the more likely they will be willing to "show their wares." Doing so is good publicity for them and could result in some future bookings for private lessons or performances at family celebrations. Many musicians double and triple on instruments of the same family, so it is often possible to provide performances on all the popular instruments using just a few performers.

Live performances by the teachers themselves are most effective, not only as part of the process but also to raise the status of the teacher in the eyes of the students. If the district music department is fortunate enough to have several teachers who play instruments from the different instrument families, the teachers can combine their forces and give a demonstration without outside help.

After the teacher performance, interested members of the audience can be invited to examine each instrument close up with the teacher/performer at hand to answer questions. An instrument display can be set up in an area where there will be enough room for the students and parents to examine the glittering brass instruments, the beautiful grained wood of the string instruments, the interesting complexity of the woodwind key systems, and the flamboyant show-biz display of the percussion section. During this time, the teacher can further explain the characteristics of the instruments and elicit comments, opinions, and levels of interest from the students. The teacher will have the opportunity to observe student interest, direction, group dynamics, and the general attitudes of those who may become members of an ensemble for as many years as they are in the school.

It is safe to say that almost every school in the United States has at least one simple computer connected to the Internet. Using that equipment, the teacher can locate YouTube performances of someone playing each instrument, review and evaluate the performance seeking the best of each, and then organize them for a showing in sequence, starting from the piccolo to the tuba, and from the violin to the double bass. Using a large viewing screen connected to an efficient sound system will help make the performances more realistic.

To ensure an interesting and fast-moving presentation, the teacher can prepare a brief but comprehensive introduction for each instrument. The potential students as a group can see and hear the instruments being played individually and then, if possible, in small or large ensembles. Using the violin as an example, a violin solo can be followed by a violin being played in a string quartet, and then in a full orchestra. For a more contemporary program, a small dance band or rock group can give an instrument-appropriate performance.

As this process evolves, each student will gravitate toward a particular category of instrument and perhaps even one in particular. It is at this point in the defined selection process that the teacher will have to begin to evaluate the physical attributes of each student to determine whether any physical limitations exist that could make playing certain instruments substantially more difficult for a given individual. It is possible that there will be situations where a student is interested in playing a particular instrument that he or she is not yet physically mature enough to handle. It is here that the measuring aspect of the defined selection process comes into place as an essential part of the total procedure. The various directions one can take to satisfy a student's choice of instrument will be discussed in chapters to follow.

Chapter Ten

The Measuring Process

Including an Annotated Directory of Modified Easy-Start Instruments

As part of the informed selection process, it is necessary for the teacher to evaluate potential students by size in relation to the instrument under consideration. If the child is very small, it is unlikely that he or she will be able to play the sousaphone as a starter instrument. If the size of a student is not in keeping with the requirements of the selected instrument, an effort should be made to find a smaller, related instrument on which the student can begin study with the intention of changing to the instrument of choice when natural growth allows. An example would be a student who desires to play the tuba starting on the baritone horn in bass clef or the euphonium.

There are numerous "modified" instruments now available that have been restructured to accommodate the growing trend to begin students of instrumental music at earlier ages. These adjustments take the form of resizing and restructuring key architecture to accommodate small hands, and adding extensions on an instrument to accommodate for shorter arm length. This chapter will describe measuring methods that have been successfully used to determine what, if any, modified instrument can be used. Those modified instruments that are currently available will be introduced with a commentary on the ways they may be used.

Measuring Nonfretted String Instruments: The Violin, Viola, Cello, and Double Bass: The growth of instrumental music education in the public schools over the past half-century has resulted in a series of modifications to instruments in all choirs. This change is most evident in the variety of sizes that have been made for nonfretted string instruments. It is now possible to obtain violins, violas, cellos, and double basses in as many as nine different sizes. Violins as small as 1/32 size increasing fractionally up to full size can easily be rented or bought from many instrument dealers. Violas, cellos, and double basses are also made in a variety of sizes so that any student can begin one of these instruments at almost any period in his or her physical development. It will be the responsibility of the teacher to accurately calculate the size of the instrument the student will need and then to keep up with the child's growth, changing sizes when required.

The following is a description of the different size nonfretted string instruments that are available today and includes some recommended procedures for evaluating a student for size.

Different-Size Violins: Because of the introduction of the Suzuki string teaching method in the mid-twentieth century, a need arose for smaller-size instruments of the violin family. The Suzuki Method begins students at the earliest possible age, in some cases even before they are able to speak. To accommodate these young people, violins are produced in nine different sizes graduated down to as small as 1/32 size. The violin sizes now available are named as follows: 4/4 = 23", 3/4 = 22", 1/2 = 20", 1/4 = 18", 1/8 = 16", 1/10 = 15", 1/16 = 14", and 1/32 = 13". One additional size that has been available for centuries is the 7/8th or "lady size" violin, which is 22 1/2". These sizes can vary slightly depending on the manufacturer.

The fractional names given to these instruments are not representative of their actual ratio to the 4/4 full-size instrument, but rather are names given to identify the various gradations. The fractional-named sizes can vary from maker to maker to as much as a half an inch in either direction. It is, therefore, recommended that the player physically try the instrument for fit, and if possible, do so under the supervision of the teacher. If that is not feasible, be sure there is a return or exchange option in the arrangement made with the dealer supplying the instrument.

Violas, cellos, and double basses have also been resized to accommodate younger students; however, the manufacturers of these instruments have not standardized the size changes and dimensions to the same degree as have violin makers. As a result, a bit more judgment is needed to determine the correct size for a young student of one of these three instruments.

Different-Size Violas: In the case of the viola, the instrument bodies are sized in inches as opposed to the system used for sizing violins. Measuring the body alone, violas graduate from a body of 12" (equal to a half-size violin), 13" (equal to a three-quarter-size violin), 14" (equal to a full-size violin), and then 15, 15 1/2, 16, and 16 1/2 inches. There are some violas that are still larger, graduating in half-inch increments up to 18", but these are usually used by professional performers. Again, be aware of the possibility of slight variations in these dimensions depending on the maker.

Often, when 12", 13", and 14" inch violas are not available, a dealer, with the approval of the teacher, will restring a half, three-quarter, or full-size violin with a viola setup to fill the need. This is a satisfactory arrangement except for the fact that the depth of those violins is a bit shallower than a viola of the same size would be. The result of this condition is a small loss of the depth of tone that is associated with the sound of a viola. In most cases in the early stages of instruction, this loss would be of little consequence and will be made up as the instrument sizes increase to true viola sizes.

Measuring for the Violin and Viola: The violin is the easiest instrument to measure for size because of the availability of the viometer. This is a device with a chin rest attached to an extendable measured tube marked at various points with violin sizes. In place of a violin, the device is placed under the student's chin using the violin playing position. The student extends the left arm straight forward with palm up. The viometer measuring rod is then extended out to reach the center of the palm of the student's hand. In that position the measuring rod will indicate the size of violin needed for the correct playing position. Viometers can be purchased online or from any music store.

The violameter is a similar device used in the same manner as the viometer. The difference is in the size indicators that are in fractions and inches for the smaller sizes and in inches only for the larger instruments. The size indicators are presented in this manner to accommodate situations where smaller than 14 1/2-inch-size violas are not available and are replaced with fractional violins restrung as violas.

If a viometer or violameter is not available, measuring for the violin and viola can be done with a tape measure. Using the playing position but without an instrument, measure the distance from the neck where the chin rest would be to the center of the palm of the hand. Be sure the arm is extended forward and straight out. The following figures indicate the appropriate size of instrument for the listed arm length.

- 14"– 15.5" = 1/16
- 15.5" – 17" = 1/10
- 17" – 18.5" = 1/8
- 18.5" – 20.5" = 1/4
- 20.5" – 22.25" = 1/2
- 22.25" – 23.5" = 3/4
- 23.5" – 24" = 7/8
- 24"+ = 4/4

The one caveat is that there is more to fitting an instrument to a child than just the arm length. A secondary but important set of subtle variants such as neck length, shape and size of the chin, and length of the fingers all play a role in fitting an instrument to a player. The bottom line here is that after the arm is measured and an appropriate size is determined, get an instrument of that size and make the final fitting. An attempt to determine the correct size on the basis of age is folly. Children of a particular age can vary in size by a foot. Age should not be a determinant.

Different-Size Cellos: Cellos, like violins, use the fraction format to identify various sizes. Unlike the consistency one finds in the sizing of violins, one will find cellos with the same-size label having different dimensions. There is a difference in body length on average of from one to three inches between what is referred to as the European measurement compared to the Suzuki measurement. The measurements for the cello body length in inches appear in table 10.1. Because of these sometimes-significant size differences, when one acquires an instrument, the player needs to physically try the instrument and, if possible, do so under the supervision of the teacher. If that is not possible, be sure that there is a return or exchange option in the arrangement made with the dealer.

Table 10.1.

Instrument Label	European Measurement	Suzuki Measurement
Full size 4/4	30 inches	30 inches
Three quarter 3/4	27 1/4 inches	26 inches
One half 1/2	26 inches	23 inches
One quarter 1/4	23 inches	20 inches
One eighth 1/8	20 inches	17 3/4 inches
One tenth 1/10	17 3/4 inches	n/a

Measuring for the Cello: There are three ways to measure a student to determine an appropriate cello size.

Using an actual cello with the end pin in the full-up position, the student should hold the instrument in playing position. It will be suspended above the floor. The correct size cello will fit as follows:

1. The heel of the neck of the cello will be at the level of the student's upper chest.
2. The top of the lower bout should be slightly above the knees.
3. The C peg should be opposite the left ear.
   If those three parts of the cello are positioned as described above, then:
4. With the student holding the cello with the knees in that position, loosen the endpin screw, drop the endpin to the floor, and tighten the screw. This will indicate the correct length for the endpin.

This process is the best and most accurate way to measure a student for a cello but it is not practical since it requires having all the different size cellos on hand.

A less accurate but more practical measuring process would be to use a tape measure to measure the student's height, arm length, and finger span. The measurements should be as follows:

- For the height, be sure the student is standing erect.
- For the arm length, measure from the tip of the middle finger to the shoulder joint.
- For the left hand with the fingers expanded as far as possible, measure from the middle of index fingernail to the middle of the pinky fingernail.

Table 10.2.   Cello Measuring Chart

Instrument Size	Height	Arm Length	Finger Span
1/4	42"–48"	18"–20"	3"–4"
1/2	49"–54"	20"–22"	4"–5"
3/4	55"–60"	22"–24"	5"–6"
4/4	60+"	24+"	6+"

The third and least effective procedure is to determine size by age, a process that I do not recommend unless there is no alternative. In this case, one will have to rely on the average size of a student of a certain age to be the guide. Generally accepted guidelines are as follows: 1/4 size for five to seven years old, 1/2 size for seven to eleven years old, 3/4 size for eleven to fifteen years old, 4/4 size for all others.

Different-Size Double Basses: The double bass has the greatest amount of latitude in the manner in which the different sizes are labeled. One would think that a full-size (4/4) double bass would be the size of choice for an adult, but that is not the case. The most commonly used bass is a three-quarter size (3/4). Unlike the violin, viola, and cello, the makers of double basses seem to enjoy a freedom in pattern design and dimension that is not available to luthiers of the smaller instruments of the violin family. An excellent illustration of this disparity in sizing is illustrated on the following website: www.gollihurmusic.com/faq/2.

Figure 10.1 illustrates the variation in double bass dimensions. The mass producers of these instruments are more inclined to adhere to some consistency of sizes in order to satisfy the needs of their customers, generally schools and younger students. Luthiers who make instruments for a specific bassist or just as a handmade instrument for sale tend to deviate from standardized sizing to achieve a specific acoustical effect.

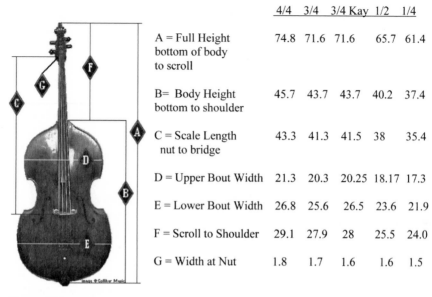

	4/4	3/4	3/4 Kay	1/2	1/4
A = Full Height bottom of body to scroll	74.8	71.6	71.6	65.7	61.4
B = Body Height bottom to shoulder	45.7	43.7	43.7	40.2	37.4
C = Scale Length nut to bridge	43.3	41.3	41.5	38	35.4
D = Upper Bout Width	21.3	20.3	20.25	18.17	17.3
E = Lower Bout Width	26.8	25.6	26.5	23.6	21.9
F = Scroll to Shoulder	29.1	27.9	28	25.5	24.0
G = Width at Nut	1.8	1.7	1.6	1.6	1.5

Figure 10.1.

Measuring for the Double Bass: Measuring a student for the double bass presents a unique set of problems. Because the industry uses a somewhat-less-rigid set of rules when designing these instruments, in some cases they may have the same size name with different string lengths or different dimensions for the body and other parts. As the sizes increase, the disparity increases, so the only really accurate way to measure a student would be to use an actual instrument, a highly unlikely situation. That being the case, proceed as follows.

It is essential that the student be able to span a whole step between the first and fourth fingers in first position on a string. When that is established, the next step would be to determine if the body of that instrument is the correct size in its totality. To make that determination, have the student stand with the right side facing the front of the double bass and the right arm in a relaxed position. Then, adjust the bass end pin out so the bridge will be even with the second knuckle of the right hand. Next, have the student put the first finger of the left hand in first position. That finger should be on the same level as the student's eye. If this is the case, the student will most likely be able to achieve proper bowing position.

It is possible to further finesse the length of the bowing arm for correct positioning on the string by about an inch and a half by using a French bow, which allows for a shorter arm, or a German bow for a longer arm. The holding position of the French bow effectively lengthens the arm by an inch and a half while the playing position of the German bow shortens the arm by the same amount. Of course, to accommodate individual differences, it is essential that some degree of flexibility be applied to all of these calculations.

Measuring for Brass Instruments: Brass instruments are not made in different sizes. The only way one can adjust for size is to select a different instrument. This situation is not as restrictive as it may appear, since brass instruments share many of the playing and fingering techniques, and some are almost identical except for size. The similarities permit an easy transition from one instrument to another, making it possible for a student to incrementally graduate to a particular instrument that may be too large to start with. The additional advantage of this incremental growth is that it allows one to experience playing several instruments on the trip up.

The Trumpet and Cornet: All B-flat trumpets and cornets are essentially the same size. One can find slight variations in weight, bore, and bell size, but these are irrelevant to the sizing issue. With very few exceptions, an average-size third-grade student can handle a trumpet or cornet. It is generally believed that the cornet has a mellower sound, although some blind tests have shown the sound of the two to be indistinguishable. In the matter of fitting the cornet for size to a player, there is no discernable difference between it and the trumpet.

A slightly smaller version of the conventional B-flat trumpet is the pocket trumpet. This instrument retains all the physical and playing characteristics of the B-flat trumpet except that the tubing that makes up the smaller instrument is more tightly configured. Should the physical size of a trumpet be an issue for a potential student, a pocket trumpet may be a solution to consider.

All the instruments in the trumpet category are fingered with the right hand. Should the use of the right hand be a problem for a student, consideration can be given to playing the French horn, which is fingered with the left hand. The section on the French horn that follows will elaborate on the playing position for that instrument.

The Flugelhorn: The flugelhorn shares all the physical characteristics of the B-flat trumpet but with a larger-size structure. The sound of the larger instrument is fuller. This larger size should be taken into consideration when one decides to start a young student on this instrument.

The French Horn: The French horn differs from the trumpet category of instruments both in size and in how it is held. In playing position, the horn is supported with the left thumb around the tubing above the valve keys and the left pinky inserted in a finger hook located on the left side of the instrument below the valve keys. On some instruments, the finger hook is adjustable, making it more player-friendly. The right hand is cupped and inserted part way into the bell, affording additional support for the instrument.

The playing position does not require that the instrument be held up and out, as one would a trumpet. There is some latitude for the angle, thereby satisfying a need for a student who is not able to hold an instrument upright for any length of time.

The French horn is fingered with the left hand. Under normal circumstances this is not usually a problem; however, if there were some physical abnormality that would preclude the use of the left hand, the French horn would not be the best choice for that student. Should such a student have a strong desire to play a French-horn-type instrument, an alternative to consider would be the mellophone, which is available in two configurations. A marching mellophone, primarily used for marching bands, looks like a big trumpet. Another style of mellophone is shaped like a French horn, sounds somewhat like a French horn, but has piston valves that are played with the right hand. Because of its overtone series, the mellophone is also much easier to play than the French horn. The mellophone is built in both E-flat and B-flat models.

The Trombone: The B-flat tenor trombone is built either as a slide or as a valve instrument. The conventional slide trombone requires the player's right arm to extend to a distance of about twenty-four inches in order to reach the lowest position. As such, the instrument is restricted to those who are of adequate size to deal with that issue.

If a student is anxious to play the slide trombone but is not yet physically mature enough to reach the lower position on the slide, there are two ways to deal with the problem. Available at little cost is a trombone slide extension, a device that can be attached to the slide, thereby shortening the distance or reach needed for the lower positions. A second solution would be to start the student on a valve trombone, which has the appearance and sound of a trombone except that there are three piston valves built into the slide design and the slide portion is stationary. When the student matures to the point where his or her arm can reach the seventh position on the slide, a transfer can be made to the slide trombone.

Background Brass: Between the trombone and the tuba are a number of lower brass instruments of various sizes. These are often referred to as background brass because they provide the background harmonies for the instruments playing the melody. The most popular of the background brasses are the alto horn, tenor horn, baritone horn, and euphonium. All of these have three or four valves and are held upright with the player in a sitting position with the instrument resting on the player's lap.

To fit any of these instruments to a player, decide which instrument is of interest, and then determine whether its size can be handled properly by sitting the potential player down with the actual instrument. Although these instruments are medium or midsize, it is their size in relation to the size of the student that is the issue. In the third grade, midsize instruments may well be too big for most students. As the grades go up, larger-size instruments can be introduced. Some of the lesser-known manufacturers make background brass instruments in smaller-than-full size. An inquiry by the teacher of some of the major music dealers and manufacturers will tell what is available.

The Tuba: The tuba is the largest brass instrument. Tubas come in several sizes, transpositions, and shapes, providing a greater opportunity for a teacher to match one with a student. Unfortunately, tubas also share the inconsistency in size classification with the double bass. Tuba sizes are classified in fractions such that a full-size tuba is called a 4/4 size, the next smaller size, 3/4, one larger than the full size is called a 5/4, and the largest of a set would be a 6/4. The system appears to show some semblance of logic until one realizes that, unlike the fractions used to classify different-size string instruments where there is some consistency, the tuba fractional sizing applies only to those instruments of a particular manufacturer. There is no consistency across brand names, so a 4/4, full-size tuba of one brand is not necessarily the same size as that of another brand. Manufacturers determine their own size dimensions. This being the case, it is in the best interest of the parties trying tubas for size not to rely on statistics but rather to have actual instruments available to try.

There are three basic designs for tubas now in popular use. The upright model, as the name implies, has an upright bell and is used for concert work. The recording model is essentially the same instrument as the upright model except for the bell, which faces forward. This instrument is often used for marching as well as for concert work. The third design is the sousaphone, named after the March King, John Phillip Sousa. This instrument is designed with the tubing turned in several concentric circles ending with the bell at the top facing forward. Because of this configuration, the player actually gets into the instrument with the tubing wrapped around the player's body.

The three models of tubas are manufactured in different sizes. In spite of these variations on the basic design and inconsistency in size, all the instruments are large and not particularly suited for a smaller child. Should a young student have a passion to play the tuba, the best direction to take would be to start on the baritone horn in bass clef and then, with some fingering adjustments, transfer to the BB-flat tuba when it becomes size-appropriate.

Measuring for Woodwind Instruments: *Note: All hand-span measurements suggested for woodwind instruments are approximate and are taken from the center of the fingernail of the subject's finger.*

Woodwind instrument have the issues of size, weight, finger span, and in some cases the size of the player's fingertips. Therefore, measuring young students for woodwind instruments requires an evaluation of the child's overall size along with a serious look at the finger span, fingertip size, and hand size. Since woodwind instruments vary in size from very small (piccolo) to very large (contrabassoon), one might consider all these different size options from which to make a choice to be an advantage. The drawback is that the different-size instruments transpose to different keys and have a different playing range, which may restrict some ensemble playing.

The Flute Family: The flute family includes many instruments, only four of which are commonly used. These are the piccolo, concert flute in C, alto flute in G, and the bass flute in C. Of these four, the concert flute in C is almost exclusively used, the piccolo second in popularity and the alto and bass only when the orchestration calls for them or if there is a need for special effects.

The size and weight of a concert C flute is not great, making the instrument easily handled by any average-size third- or fourth-grade student. For very young children, the main issue to consider is their finger span. Reaching all the keys comfortably on the C flute requires a span of about three inches from the index finger to the pinky on the left hand and three and a half inches for the same fingers on the right hand. If the student cannot comfortably span the keys, there is the likelihood that reaching for a key will cause an embouchure change affecting tone production.

Another consideration in measuring one for playing the flute is the distance from the lip plate and embouchure hole where the lips are placed to the first key articulated by the first finger of the left hand. This distance is approximately ten inches and can be a problem for a small child to reach comfortably enough to finger the notes easily. Should this be the case, the solution lies in the use of a curved U-shaped head joint, which significantly shortens the distance between the embouchure hole and the first key on the instrument's body. The curved head joint is made by several manufacturers and is often brand-interchangeable. If one is to purchase this item separately, it is best to bring the flute that is to be used to the point of purchase to be sure of the fit.

An additional option for the small beginner is the Wave-Line head joint, which has a U-shaped dip in the center of the head joint rather than having the entire head joint in a U shape. The manufacturer claims that this configuration distributes the weight more evenly throughout the instrument. With this head joint, the distance between the embouchure hole and the first key is shortened.

One might think that a smaller player would be better off starting on the piccolo because of its diminutive size, but this is not necessarily true. The embouchure needed to play the piccolo is very compressed, whereas a C flute embouchure is more relaxed, and easier to achieve. Playing the piccolo is best attempted after one has achieved a reasonable degree of proficiency on the C flute.

The alto and bass flutes present a different set of problems. Because of their larger size and the comparatively large size of the embouchure hole in the head joint, beginning players may have a difficult time dealing with them. In addition to the larger reach, a great deal more airflow is required to generate a sound. If there is a need to introduce these instruments to a program, it is probably best to postpone doing so and wait for a time when the players have developed a reasonable degree of proficiency on the C flute.

The Clarinet Family: The B-flat soprano clarinet is the instrument in the clarinet family most often played and used to start a new student. The span needed for the left-hand index finger to the pinky is approximately 2 3/4 inches. The span is 3 1/2 inches for the same fingers in the right hand.

An additional consideration is the padding of the student's fingertips. Clarinets have open tone-holes that are played using ringed, open-hole keys. This means that the six holes on the front of the clarinet and one on the back are not covered by padded keys. These must be covered by the player's fingertips. The issues to be evaluated are whether the young person's fingertips have sufficiently fleshy padding to securely cover the instrument's open tone-holes and whether the finger span is great enough to reach all the keys. The student must be able to reach the pinky keys while maintaining proper placement and completely covering the open tone-holes. Because it is essential that all these requirements be met, it would be best to actually use an instrument as the measuring device to determine if a very small child is able to manage this key configuration.

Should the potential student not be able to meet the physical requirements needed to play a B-flat soprano clarinet but still wishes to do so, there are several instruments that can be used as a temporary measure to get the studies started. One option is a clarinet that is built with plateau keys. These are cup-shaped keys similar to those on a flute that contain pads that cover the traditional open tone-hole ring keys on a clarinet. Available by several manufacturers, these instruments have all the acoustical and mechanical characteristics of the traditional B-flat soprano clarinet with plateau keys in place of the open tone-hole keys. Using these instruments, the player is not required to cover an open-hole key completely. The pad does the job. In the opinion of some experts, this key design alters the sound of the clarinet to some degree since the plateau keys modify the acoustical principles required to produce the best tone on the instrument. This may be true; however, I believe that the shortcoming is of little consequence at this point in a beginning student's career.

The Kinder Klari clarinet is a small E-flat clarinet with a modified key system. The instrument replicates an actual clarinet in appearance and sound and has keys that are designed to facilitate use by one with smaller hands. The Kinder Klari has eleven keys, and claims to be 40 percent smaller and 36 percent lighter than a traditional B-flat clarinet. The one possible drawback to using this instrument is the transposition, which is in E-flat. This restricts the player's inclusion in certain ensemble work.

Another solution to a small hand problem is to use a traditional E-flat sopranino clarinet, which is smaller than a B-flat soprano clarinet. This instrument has traditional open-hole keys and the advantage of a smaller size, but produces a somewhat different timbre, is more expensive to buy, and is considered by some to be a bit more difficult to play. Perhaps this is not the best choice for small hands.

Should the new player not be suited for any of the instruments mentioned here but still want to start on a clarinet, an instrument called the Clarineo or the Lyons C Clarinet has a modified fully chromatic Boehm key system that covers the entire range of a traditional B-flat clarinet but is a C instrument. It is lightweight (about one-third as heavy as a B-flat clarinet), waterproof, and easily repaired with replacement keys. Since it is a C instrument, it can be used to double the parts of any other C instrument such as the flute or violin. However, if it is to be used to play a traditional B-flat clarinet part in an ensemble, transposition will be necessary.

The choices then come down to not playing the clarinet, trying to play it with inadequate finger span (not a particularly wise choice), or starting study using one of the smaller instruments for a period of time until the student grows enough to transfer to a B-flat soprano clarinet. If the student is not of sufficient size to handle the instrument, the third choice is recommended.

The Saxophone Family: There are five instruments in the saxophone family that are in popular use. In order of popularity, they are the alto, tenor, baritone, soprano, and bass. With the exception of the soprano, the other four saxophones increase in size from large to very large and are considerably heavier than the other instruments of the woodwind family. These instruments are not suitable for a small beginner. The span needed in the left hand for an alto saxophone from index finger to pinky is about 3 3/4 inches, and for the same fingers on the right hand, about four inches.

One of the difficulties in using the saxophone key system exists with the side keys, which are located on both sides of the instrument and are activated by side motion of each hand. When one plays the saxophone, it is necessary for these keys to remain untouched while the index, middle, and third fingers are articulating the six front keys. For this to happen, a player's fingers must be long enough for the thumb to remain on the back of the instrument while the other fingers reach around to articulate the keys on the front of the instrument without touching the side keys. This does not preclude the saxophone from being introduced in the early grades, but it means that careful evaluation of the physical size of the potential student should be initiated before a saxophone is selected.

The saxophones that are smaller and lighter than the alto are the sopranissimo in B-flat, the sopranino in E-flat, and the soprano in B-flat. The sopranissimo and sopranino are not particularly easy to come by, are expensive, and are not easily incorporated into a beginning instrumental music class because of their range and key transposition. The soprano in B-flat sounds a fifth above the alto and would require transposed music if it were to be played with other saxophones. These instruments have the same key systems as their larger cousins and share many of the same fingering problems.

The tenor and baritone saxophones are very large instruments. Unless a beginner is physically mature enough to handle their size, it is best to postpone introducing them as a doubling instrument to the alto at some later time.

One solution to dealing with the size and weight of the saxophone can be found with the E-flat Alphasax. This instrument is designed to satisfy the need for a saxophone that can be handled by a smaller student. The Alphasax is 33 percent lighter than the traditional E-flat alto sax and features a traditional body with a key mechanism designed to accommodate the smaller hand. The mechanism enables the player to articulate a full two octaves chromatically using traditional fingering patterns, allowing the young student to easily prepare for a transition to a traditional sax when possible.

The Oboe: The process of fitting a young student for an oboe is dependent on the instrument that is going to be used. Oboes can have a plateau key system or an open tone-hole system. The plateau keys on an oboe are similar to those described in the clarinet section above. They have cup-shaped keys containing pads that cover the open tone-holes. These are easier for young people to use since in most cases the key simply needs to be depressed rather than having the player actually cover an open hole with the padding of the fingertips. There is a modification to that process that takes place when certain notes being fingered require a half-hole fingering; however, those situations do not usually present a problem for beginning players.

Oboes are not particularly heavy, nor are they difficult to handle, but they are difficult to play. More on that later! The dimensions needed for the player's span from the index finger to the pinky are three and half inches for both hands.

If the instrument has an open tone-hole key system, consideration must also be given to composition of the player's fingertips: There must be sufficient flesh on them to completely cover the open tone-hole while articulating the thumb and side keys on the instrument. The slightest air leak will result in a squawk. Consequently, the safest route would be to use a plateau key instrument if possible.

The Bassoon: The bassoon should be reserved for a fully mature student who, in the teacher's judgment, is tall enough and strong enough to deal with handling the instrument and its case, adept enough to assemble the instrument, and possesses sufficient finger span to articulate the keys. There are numerous key systems for bassoons. All are built with a labyrinth of keys and open tone holes. Playing this instrument requires two fully mature hands with at least average-length fingers. A bassoon can contain as many as thirteen thumb keys alone. These are articulated with both thumbs, while the other four fingers on each hand are dealing with the open tone-holes, spatula keys, occasional half-hole requirements and numerous side keys. No easy task.

The span from the index finger to the pinky on the left hand is generally four inches, with the same fingers on the right hand needing a span of four and a half inches. Should a student have this span, it is advisable that the actual instrument be used to test the entire handling and fingering requirements before a decision is made on the selection of this instrument.

Measuring for Percussion Instruments: Percussion instruments offer an abundance of choices for any size player. This category of instruments produces sound by reacting to any type of agitation such as being struck, scraped, blown into, or, in the case of something with sound-producing particles in an enclosed vessel, shaken. Unlike the instruments of the other families that require very accurate finger placement and allow for little or no latitude, one can find a percussion instrument that will be suitable in size for any individual. From the triangle to the marimba to the bass drum, the percussion section offers an opportunity for inclusion of students at any point in their physical development. The most practical process for evaluating a student for size to play a percussion instrument should consist of a one-on-one teacher-student personal interview in the presence of all the percussion instruments available so an appropriate decision can be made for the student.

Chapter Eleven

The Dealer/Teacher Relationship

All school music programs have some school-owned instruments. Depending on the size of the program, the faculty, and the protocol established by the administration, periodically someone will have the responsibility of purchasing instruments, music, and supplies. Any wise dealer knows that a teacher can be the hub around which innumerable sales can be generated for years and even decades. Since this is the case, a dealer should make every effort to provide for a teacher's specific needs.

The wise teacher can use that position of strength to his or her benefit; however, there is a danger of overplaying that hand. The fact that the dealer wants to create an affiliation and lock in an ongoing relationship with a teacher does not necessarily imply that the teacher has an open season on the dealer. The following are some guidelines for teachers and dealers that will help both parties understand each other's point of view and in so doing help ensure a successful relationship.

The Dealer's Role: The dealer should make clear to the teachers and general public the range of services being offered. These services ought to include instrument sales, rentals, and repairs, the sale of printed music, accessories, and any other music products and services related to the music programs in the immediate geographical area. If there are any restrictions or omissions, it would be best to make them known in advance. All policies concerning the terms of sales and services should be publically displayed. These policies include guarantees, warrantees, refund policies, hours of operation, and any other information that will facilitate and encourage consumers to use that service with confidence.

As a primary support system for any music program, there will be times when a service required will be a financial loss to the dealer. This should be undertaken with the same courtesy and efficiency accorded a high-profit-yielding transaction. Such an approach will be a guarantee of success and profit in the long run.

The company's owner and staff must be fully informed in all areas in which services are offered. If instruments from all families are offered for sale, rent, or repair, it is incumbent on the dealer to have fully qualified technicians on hand to attend to the maintenance and repair of those instruments. This can be accomplished by either having such a staff available in-store if the volume of business warrants it or, at the very least, having an arrangement with experienced professional technicians or luthiers to provide the needed services promptly.

If printed music is offered, the dealer should make every effort to learn from the teachers the anticipated needs of their program and then take whatever steps necessary to have that material available within a reasonable time. An additional much-appreciated service for teachers would be to provide a periodic update about new publications and arrangements relevant to the grade levels being taught. This can be efficiently accomplished on a dealer's website and by e-mail updates to the teachers.

The same service should be provided for accessories and supplies with consideration given to products that are specific to each teacher. Such items as a special-size mouthpiece, a particular brand of reeds or strings, or a certain pitch pipe, metronome, or chin rest fall into this category. A reasonable inventory of the more popular items should be maintained to avoid the consumer's frustration that accompanies out-of-stock items.

It is impossible for most dealers to stock the myriad accessories, instruments, and printed matter available on the market. But knowing where and how to get almost anything is not an unreasonable expectation to have for a conscientious dealer. The Internet does it all. But it does so for all for teachers as well, giving them the opportunity to purchase anything online, and often at a lower price. The advantage the local dealer has over the Internet is service and availability. The challenge for the dealer is to be prepared, able, and willing to tend to the teacher's needs expeditiously and courteously.

Most music companies will provide a delivery service to the schools at a day and time prearranged with the teacher. It is important and expected that the dealer be prompt and consistent in providing this service, since the teacher relies on receiving the products in that delivery to advance the music program. Dependability is the keynote to success in this instance.

The Teacher's Role: A dealer who expects to earn a living from his business will try to fulfill his or her responsibilities to the highest degree possible. But there are two sides to that coin. The teacher also has a responsibility to ensure that the relationship between the two is amicable by maintaining a reasonable level of expectation regarding all phases of the services while maintaining a respect for the dealer's efforts. Both parties should conduct their activities in a manner that would encourage mutual success. A music program cannot survive without equipment and services. The dealer who can provide the equipment and services efficiently with respect for the customer and at a competitive price is a very valuable asset to a music program. The following are some ways a teacher can contribute to the dealer-teacher relationship.

Just as positive reinforcement is a valuable tool in the classroom, that approach can also be effective in advancing the relationship with a dealer and in so doing encourage enthusiastic service. Luciano Pavarotti once said after a performance, "The applause is my oxygen." This is probably true of all types of applause. A pat on the back when warranted is always welcomed. Conversely, any improprieties or errors should be reported to the dealer directly, courteously, and expeditiously. It is never wise to tell a third party to tell the dealer about a problem because the message will inevitably be transmitted, if accurately at all, in a less-than-productive style. "The teacher said to tell you . . ." will always end in some form of hyperbole, whereas a direct message via e-mail, phone, or a personal visit from the teacher will invariably resolve the problem quickly and without any unnecessary ill feelings. Public criticism is not a good idea. Keep all complaints impersonal and directed privately to the dealer.

In anticipation of the upcoming year's program, an experienced teacher will try to determine in advance the music and supplies that will be needed. An efficient dealer will be happy to stock that merchandise before the beginning of the school year to help ensure a fast and smooth school opening. With that arrangement, it is incumbent on the teacher to make every effort to be accurate in estimating both the quantities and items in the request. If a teacher tells the dealer to stock seventy-five of a particular lesson book and buys only thirty, the dealer is stuck with the remaining forty-five books. They will remain on the shelf for at least a year or, should the teacher change books in the next year, the dealer will be stuck with the books indefinitely. There goes the profit and with enough of those bad moves, the dealership.

Most repairs require a trained technician, time, tools, and materials to be properly executed. Occasionally, a small adjustment will do the trick. But that, too, requires experienced personnel to perform the job. Although it is sometimes possible for the dealer's field representative or delivery person to make on-the-spot repairs, it is not reasonable for a teacher to expect such a service.

One of the major problems dealers are confronted with much too frequently is nonpayment of invoices for work or products already provided. The scenario is usually one where a purchase order that has been filled sits in the business office waiting for the teacher to confirm the completion of the transaction. It is not uncommon for a dealer who has filled an order to have to wait months to be paid for a service that had to be paid for on the dealer's end within thirty days. Included in that situation are salaries of the employees, which are paid within in a week or two, while the funds required to cover those expenses are months away.

The problem is usually the result of the teacher's not feeling personally responsible for the bill payment when, in fact, the final responsibility does rest with the teacher. School districts usually have a procedure for the teacher to follow that will set the payment process in motion. Some consideration on the teacher's part would always be greatly appreciated by the dealer. Think of how it would feel if the teacher's salary checks were distributed at the convenience of the administration!

The symbiotic relationship between the dealer and music teacher is essential to the survival of both parties. A good dealer who is efficient, reliable, and knowledgeable is a very valuable but, unfortunately, not very common asset. If a teacher is lucky enough to find one, it would be advantageous to treat him or her with respect and courtesy and encourage an atmosphere of cooperation. Both parties are working toward the same goal of building and supporting the music program being served. If the teacher requests a service, it should be provided expeditiously. Even if that request is beyond the bounds of routine service, every effort should be made by the dealer to accommodate that need. Under such circumstances, reasonableness should be the rule on both sides.

Chapter Twelve

Buying Instruments for School Use

Note: Some information from the previous chapters will be repeated in the buying sections for the convenience of the reader.

The Process: School districts have procedures outlined for the purchase of all supplies and equipment. Musical instruments and supplies can be purchased directly from a dealer with a school purchase order using school funds. Occasionally, parents' and local citizens' largesse will result in contributions of instruments or money to a program.

Some districts require purchases be open to the bidding process for which the district will have a format to follow. This process allows any qualified dealer to bid with the intention of the school achieving the lowest price. There can, however, be unintended consequences to this process: The lowest price is not always accompanied by reliability and a professional support system. Promises are not always kept.

In any case, it is the teacher's responsibility to oversee every detail of the process. Among the issues to be considered are researching the specifications of the instruments or equipment to be purchased, implementing the buying process in a manner that will result in the best possible results monetarily and in the quality of products purchased, insuring that the supplier will serve the needs of the program, and having a support system to back up those products. This is no easy task.

Buying Instruments: Shopping for a school musical-instrument program usually involves buying string, woodwind, brass, and percussion instruments in large quantities. It is therefore necessary for the buyer to establish an instrument-evaluation procedure that will be general enough to cover those attributes that are common to all instruments, accompanied by a more specific agenda that will apply to the unique characteristics of each instrument. The process should consist of the following steps:

1. Determine the program's needs based on the curriculum, number of students, instrumentation, inventory on hand, replacements needed, and desired increase in the inventory. Make it a wish list that will then be adjusted as the budget is brought into play.
2. Decide what quality level of instruments is needed. Instruments are usually classified as beginner or student level, intermediate, advanced, and professional level. Of course, anyone would want to buy the very best, but in almost every case that is neither practical nor possible. Since this is the case, the next step would be to determine whether it is necessary to purchase any instrument above the student level. This is an individual decision that must be based first on finances. If money is not an issue, then proceed up the ladder as far as the allotted funds will permit.
3. Establish the budget to include a distribution of the funds that will best provide for the needs of the program while remaining within the monetary limitations.
4. Begin the search for brands, models, and prices of instruments that will fulfill the requirements of numbers 2 and 3 above. This will require patience, investigative curiosity, and tenacity. (See "The Search" section later in this chapter for some help in this area.)
5. Based on the findings thus far, use realistic estimated prices to calculate the cost of the "dream" purchase. At this point, it may be advantageous to discuss pricing with a local dealer, consult the Internet, and also consult a nonlocal dealer to get an outside opinion. This assortment of opinions will expand the buyer's knowledge and give a better overall picture of the market.
6. Determine how the calculated cost fits into the allotted budget.
7. If it fits, you're set. If it doesn't, proceed to step 8.
8. Begin to reduce the dream purchase by prioritizing the importance of the instruments being considered. If there are any upgrade instruments in the plan, reduce them to the next-lower-priced instrument. If all the proposed purchases are student level with no opportunity to downgrade, try cutting back on the instrument that has the largest quantity in the order. Instead of six, buy five. The proviso here is that such a cut will not have a significantly deleterious effect on the program. It is better to have fewer of some instruments than none of another.
9. Tally up the cost, be sure it fits in the budget, and then recalculate the estimated costs to confirm that the original estimates were realistic and not a dream for this order.

The Search: The ultimate aim in a search for all instruments is to find those that will best serve the program and enable the players to produce the best sound. Consideration has to be given to an instrument's tone quality and pitch accuracy. Other considerations are ease of handling; weight, size, finish, and workmanship; the fit of moving parts such as valves, slides, and pegs; materials used in the construction; and an awareness of any anomalies peculiar to each instrument. All instruments share some of the same features, but do so in different ways requiring significantly different procedures to be properly evaluated.

Summary: In some circumstances, a buyer will be seeking his or her major instrument and will be well qualified to make a reasonable evaluation of the subject instrument. In the case of a teacher who is charged with purchasing a variety of instruments, some of which are not his or her major, the challenge can be to evaluate nonmajor instruments from any or all of the four choirs. Under these circumstances one must devise a generalized evaluation model that can be applied to the selection of instruments from all choirs regardless of the buyer's areas of expertise. This paradigm along with any outside assistance should result in a successful purchase.

Selecting instrument brands and models requires due diligence on the highest level. When given the responsibility to purchase instruments that are outside of one's area of expertise, it is incumbent on the buyer to make every effort to educate him- or herself to the highest level possible. How to proceed? In a word, conscientiously. This is a multifaceted mission requiring research and patience. Some advice on what to look for and how to find it will follow.

When evaluating instruments that are not in the shopper's area of expertise, begin by seeking advice from any authority in the subject instrument. Knowledgeable individuals would include other teachers, performers, manufacturers, experienced successful dealers, repair technicians, and certainly, the Internet. Some general evaluation procedures can be applied to the purchase of all instruments. One must acquire knowledge of the product lines and pricing of the entire range of offerings on the market. It is not uncommon for a major manufacturer to offer a dozen models of trumpets ranging from a student model for $200 to a professional model for $2,000, with ten different models in between. One will find a number of manufacturers of the same instrument offering enough different models to boggle the mind. At this writing, the Schilke Company offers sixteen trumpet models on the Internet. Conn, Yamaha, Beuscher, Olds, Holton, Bach, and Getzen are just some of the more established brands of trumpets whose manufacturers also offer numerous models. Concurrent with these major manufacturers are a number of smaller, lesser-known makers, importers, and specialized hand craftsmen who produce trumpets. Where does one start? The following chapters will deal with instruments from each of the four instrument families individually.

Chapter Thirteen

Buying String Instruments

The Violin, Viola, Cello, and Double Bass

Choosing a string instrument to buy is a challenge for even the most astute and experienced musician. Because instruments in the violin family are made of wood, a reactive substance, and have an architecture that in combination with the wood is conducive to extraordinary individuality, each of these instruments is its own person.

One can play six trumpets in succession of the same brand and model and find each with some slight differences, but generally they will all respond in like manner. This will be the case with most items fabricated of manufactured material. It is possible to make a substance such as fiberglass in large quantities that will have a consistent basic structure. Fiberglass bows of the same model and manufacturer are generally very much the same. Natural wood does not share that characteristic. Each piece of wood is unique, so each instrument made from a piece of wood has its own individuality. The search for an instrument then becomes a matter of having exposure to as many instruments of the kind being sought as possible.

Violins, violas, cellos, and double basses can be bought for almost any price and in any quality. When searching for one of these instruments to purchase, the process should include a careful evaluation of the attributes of the instruments that fall into the predetermined price range while providing for the needs of the school program. An understanding of the qualities to look for and how to recognize them along with a realistic understanding of how likely one's expectations are to be fulfilled in the price range allotted must be part of the buyer's preparation prior to beginning the search.

Violins, violas, cellos, and double basses that are manufactured and marketed by brand name most often have a manufacturer's recommended retail price and sport a price tag. If you have selected such an instrument, you have a point of reference from which you can proceed to bargain. In the major metropolitan areas, it is not uncommon to get a discount of between 30 and 40 percent off that manufacturer's recommended retail price. Those discounts are entirely up to the dealer and the immediate market in which the instrument is being sold.

Pragmatism must be an important part of the decision-making process. The following are some hints on how to proceed.

1. Price: Determine a spending price range with a span of about $300 (e.g., $100–400, $500–800, $900–1,200). Keep in mind that although it is possible to buy a violin or viola for a hundred dollars, it will more than likely be worthless. Also, one must accept the fact that a hundred-dollar cello or double bass of any musical value does not exist.

2. Old vs. New: Buying upgraded older string instruments for a school music program is probably not a good idea unless the intention is to provide for the needs of advanced players who would appreciate the value of such an instrument. If that is indeed the case, then the selection process should be handled by a person who is knowledgeable in that area. The instruments should be selected and evaluated on an individual basis. Bulk purchases or job lots will invariably include some duds.

There are many theories and opinions on whether new or old is the better choice. Some commonly held opinions are as follows:

- A bad new or bad old string instrument will always be bad, so avoid those. You will learn how to do so in the following pages.
- A good new instrument, if properly cared for, will become a better instrument as it is played and the wood ages.
- An old good string instrument, depending on its age, will probably not improve as much as a new one since it has most likely already done so.
- What to do? Try them all, and try to find the instrument that will best suit the needs of the greater percentage of your student body.

3. Take a Good Look: The following suggestions can be applied to both new and older instruments. New instruments should be damage-free and conform to all of the setup and adjustment qualifications described below. Check for warping, cracks, and a proper setup for the bridge. For an older instrument, check the interior and exterior for cracks, open seams, chips, dents, or scratches and evidence of any kind of repair. Keep in mind that chips, dents, or scratches do not necessarily affect the performance of an instrument, but they do affect the value.

Inside: A look inside what is offered as an old instrument will show if, in fact, it really is old. Luthiers are very skilled at making the exterior of a new instrument look old, but the inside will tell the story. If the wood on the inside of the instrument is light in color, new, and fresh in appearance, it is likely to be new. Old instruments are old both inside and out. It is more difficult for a luthier to artificially age the inside of an instrument than to do so for the outside.

Repairs: A properly repaired crack or re-glued seam is acceptable; however, a repaired crack can lower the value of an instrument. The operative word here is *properly*. A proper crack repair should be difficult to spot and almost if not completely smooth to the touch. Close your eyes and pass your finger across the repaired crack. You should feel almost no evidence of a repair.

The next step is to examine the neck and fingerboard of the instrument. The neck should be free of cracks and smooth to the touch on the underside. This portion of the instrument is generally not finished as is the body but rather oiled and hand-rubbed to provide a smooth surface for the player's hand to slide up and down the various positions.

In some better-quality older instruments, one may see a splice where the neck joins the body. On an old good instrument, the splice may be an indication of the neck angle correction or even of the neck having been replaced to accommodate contemporary strings. This can be a good indication that the instrument was considered by someone in the past to be worthy of this type of alteration. Unfortunately, this splice is sometimes put on a newer instrument to deceive the buyer into thinking it is an old instrument of good quality.

New instruments should be damage-free and conform to all of the setup and adjustment qualifications described below.

Warping: While holding the instrument in such a position as to be able to look down the fingerboard from the pegbox toward the bridge, check to be sure the fingerboard is smooth, true, and not warped. If there is any buzzing when a string is plucked or bowed, that is an indication of a possibly warped fingerboard or an improperly fitted nut. The space between the string and fingerboard at the point of the nut should be sufficient to allow the string to vibrate easily but not so high as to be uncomfortable for the player.

Setup: The term *setup* refers to the manner in which the strings rest on the nut at the top of the fingerboard and travel down the fingerboard and over the bridge to be connected to the tailpiece. Although it is possible to present some measurements for general reference, the final dimensions are peculiar to each instrument. A proper setup will have a bridge that is arched to allow the four strings to be easily bowed individually or in conjunction with one another when playing double stops. The slots in which the strings are placed on the bridge should be only as deep as is necessary to prevent the strings from moving horizontally. To achieve optimum sound, the bridge should be positioned so that its feet are in direct alignment with the notches visible in the center of the inside of the f holes.

Bridge: When viewing an instrument's bridge from its side, one should ensure that the side of the bridge facing the tailpiece is flat and at a perfect 90-degree angle from the top of the instrument. The fingerboard side of the bridge should be graduated to a smaller thickness toward its top. The illusion is that the bridge appears to be leaning toward the tailpiece. This configuration is intended to compensate for the tendency of a bridge to warp in the direction of the fingerboard as a result of the strings being pulled toward the fingerboard when tuning.

After checking to see that the bridge is properly centered between the two notches on the sides of the f holes, one should look down the fingerboard from the pegbox again to check the alignment of the strings. They should travel in a direct line from the pegbox over the nut, over the fingerboard, over the bridge, and to the tailpiece.

Pegs: Pegs on a violin, viola, and cello hold the strings in tune and must be properly installed if they are to work effectively. They must turn smoothly and remain firmly in place when the instrument is tuned. The pegs should be installed with the ears extending a comfortable distance out from the pegbox and so that the opposite end of the peg is flush with the outside of the pegbox. The peg ends should not protrude from the pegbox.

The hole in the peg through which the string is threaded should be close to the narrow end of the peg. This is necessary in order to allow the string to wind around the peg smoothly and progress concentrically away from the hole toward the center of the peg. Although other woods and synthetic products are sometimes used, pegs are most often made of rosewood or ebony. It is recommended that the pegs be made of a hard wood if they are to stay in place.

As stated previously, the space between the string and the fingerboard at the nut should be enough to allow the string to vibrate easily and yet not so great as to be uncomfortable for the player. If the slot in the nut is too deep, the open string will buzz. If the nut is too high, the player will feel uncomfortable when depressing a string.

Top: A comparison of several instruments will show some variation in the arch or bulge of the center of the top as compared to its sides. It is generally believed that instruments with higher arches tend to produce a more assertive or nasal tone as compared to those with flatter arching. Often, instruments whose arches are higher are lower in price than a comparable instrument with a lower arch. Additionally, those older, higher-arched instruments have increased in value less than that of their flatter counterparts. The final choice should still be the instrument that satisfies most of the requirements of the player.

Finish: Look beyond the finish of the instrument into the wood grain. A variety of woods are used in making string instruments. For an instrument to perform properly, its different parts require different strengths and resonance responses to make up the whole sound-producing device. Although there are exceptions, traditionally spruce is used for the top, the blocks, and the linings. Maple is used for the sides, back, neck, and scroll, and ebony for the pegs, fingerboard, tailpiece, and end button. Woods other than spruce, maple, and ebony can be used. The most common substitute is boxwood in place of ebony parts. For less-expensive instruments, the ebony parts are replaced with other inexpensive hardwood that is stained or painted black.

Purfling: Purfling is the inlay of two thin strips of hardwood that surrounds the edge of the body of a string instrument. The purfling is recessed into the edge of the top and back plates to the depth of about a sixteenth of an inch on a violin and proportionately deeper for the larger instruments. The exact depth is determined by the luthier. The function of purfling is to reinforce the edges of the instrument to prevent chipping and cracking. Purfling is also used by more sophisticated luthiers to control the vibration of the wood and in so doing to modify the sound production.

The degree of perfection with which the purfling has been installed can also be a measure of the luthier's skills. The most difficult part of the purfling to install is the point at the tip of each bout where the two strips meet. Instruments of a lesser quality will have a parallel line painted in place of a real inlay.

Scroll: The scroll of an instrument is also an indication of the maker's skills. On the better instruments, one can easily see the finesse of craftsmanship and the luthier's personal adaptation of the basic scroll shape. At first glance by the nonprofessional, all scrolls look about the same. When one places several instruments side by side, an examination will quickly show how they differ. The quality and individuality of a scroll is interesting to observe and can add to or detract from the aesthetic appeal of the instrument. However, it should not be a significant factor in the final selection.

Wood Grain: There is some difference of opinion about the importance of the grain of the wood of a violin, viola, cello, or double bass. It is certainly important to the appearance of an instrument, where a beautiful piece of well-grained wood is a definite plus. The question of the effect of the grain on sound production arises when one sees the instruments made by Stradivari and Amati. Although some of these highly prized instruments were fabricated of beautifully grained woods, others were not. Yet the less-attractive instruments are as highly rated as their more attractive siblings. One must conclude that it is the inherent structure of the wood, rather than its grain alone, combined with the workmanship of the luthier that are the significant factors in an instrument's ultimate sound production.

Finish: String-instrument bodies are finished with spirit- (alcohol) based or oil- (petroleum) based varnish or, on less-expensive instruments, with lacquer to protect the wood. History abounds with speculation concerning the importance of the varnish from the past and its effect on the sound of the instruments. As of 2014, however, no conclusion has been reached on the validity of those theories. That being said, the substance used to finish an instrument can affect the sound if that product tends to dry to a ridged state or if it has been applied too thickly. The optimum application should be of sufficient clarity and flexibility as to not impede the vibration of the wood.

4. Play the Instrument: The next step, and the most important one in selecting an instrument from the violin family, is to hear the instrument under consideration and to feel how it responds to the player. This phase of the evaluation process is the most subjective, since all of the instrument's responses will be judged on the basis of a player's previous musical experiences, musical taste, ability to perform, and ability to discern minute yet significant differences in the sounds being produced.

Violin-family instruments are as unique as human beings, so when a person begins to search for the one unique instrument that will satisfy his or her needs and expectations, the search itself becomes unique. One person can prefer filet of sole, and another, filet mignon. Both satisfy hunger and provide protein-rich nourishment. Which is better? Neither. They are different foods and satisfy different individual tastes. Such is the case with string instruments. The choice is individual and totally subjective. Entirely different products can be successful candidates for different individuals.

Judging: Judging an instrument for its productivity is a very complex process. Sound and an instrument's potential to provide it are made up of many diverse components. The most important is the synergy among the instrument's capacity to respond, the bow being used, and the player's ability to maximize that potential.

Amplitude: The first step in evaluating an instrument's sound should consist of listening for amplitude—the volume of sound the instrument can produce. A concurrent consideration is the instrument's ability to project the sound in a manner that sustains or resonates sufficiently to carry on to the next note but not so much as to confuse subsequent sounds.

To evaluate an instrument's amplitude, start by bowing each individual open string. Use a strong, separate, down-bow stroke, releasing the bow from the string immediately to allow it to resound. Repeat the process for each string, listening to the resonance of the sound and measuring the duration of that sound after the bow leaves the string. Better instruments will resound longer; lesser instruments will resound shorter. Proceed to use the same process with a progression of fingered notes on each string to hear how the instrument responds to that action. Now go through the same process using pizzicato, plucking the string and allowing it to resonate. A responsive instrument should continue to resound after each note is plucked.

Tone Quality: The question of tone quality, also a very subjective characteristic, should be considered next. General terms used to identify sounds are *bright, dark, mellow, harsh, aggressive, warm*, and *full-bodied*, among others. To make a sound judgment, no pun intended, one must first test the four open strings. Play them with long, legato bowing with a volume ranging from *ppp* to *fff*. Close your eyes and concentrate on the quality of the sound you hear. If the sound pleases you, that's the instrument for you. Keep that instrument on the A list and continue as follows.

Balance: The next important element one must consider is the consistency with which the instrument produces that sound quality on the four different strings and in the seven possible positions that can be played on the instrument. Compare the sound produced on each string with that produced on the other strings. Balance, that is, equal ability to produce sound across the strings, is a measure of a good instrument. Ideally, the strings should perform with consistent splendor at every point on the instrument. Such a result is not very likely, but the closer one comes to it, the better.

Procedure: The most effective way to hear the true sound of an instrument is to play a simple major scale slowly with full bow strokes starting from the lowest open string in first position and proceeding up into all seven positions. It is most unlikely that one will find all pitches producing equally, but, again, the closer the balance of sound of the notes to one another, the better. If the player is satisfied with the instrument thus far, it is then time to play it in every way possible, using exercises and music of every kind. If the instrument feels comfortable and produces to the expectations of the player, things are going well.

Bearing in mind that a string instrument sounds different to the player than to a listener, the best test would be to have someone other than the principal player play the instrument. The person doing the selecting should try to listen to the instrument from every possible distance and vantage point. If you're satisfied, buy it.

Chapter Fourteen

Buying a Bow

Selecting and buying a bow can be as difficult as doing so for an instrument, but with a different set of challenges. The good news is a bow has fewer parts to evaluate. The process is simpler for a beginner's bow than for an upgraded model.

The phrase "good instrument + bad bow = bad sound" summarizes the issue in the simplest terms. A bow should be matched to the instrument for which it will be used. Like any item, bows are available at every quality level from junk to magnificent. The factors to be evaluated are the material from which the stick is made, the kind of hair it has, the balance of the bow, its camber (degree of curve), the stability of the frog; the bow's ease of movement, and finally, any cosmetic adornments if present or desired.

The Stick: The stick of a bow is its spine. It can be made of almost any wood or certain manufactured substances such as carbon fiber or fiberglass. For wooden bows, the preference is pernambuco wood, an increasingly rare and expensive choice. A second choice would be a high-grade Brazilwood. The term *Brazilwood* is used rather loosely and can mean any kind of wood grown in Brazil. The country of origin is not a guarantee of quality because, obviously, any kind of wood can come from Brazil. Therefore, it is essential that a wood other than pernambuco be of a high quality.

Carbon fiber and fiberglass bows have advanced in quality and design to the point where they are considered by many to be perfectly acceptable replacements for wood. Fiberglass bow sticks with horsehair are comparatively low-priced and durable, do not warp, and are widely used for beginning students. Carbon fiber bows are available in many price levels, some ranging to $500 and more. These are excellent substitutes for wooden bows and, if these are being considered, they should be put through the same tests as those for a wooden bow.

When inspecting a wooden bow stick, look for a consistently dense grain free of imperfections, knots, or blemishes. It should be strong yet flexible, and resilient enough to bend easily, but not so much as to contact the hair while playing or bend to either side to any great degree.

Camber is the curve in a bow stick. Check the degree of curve with the bow hair loose. Then tighten the hair until it is about one quarter of an inch from the center of the stick at the midpoint of the bow. This will approximate playing tension. Examine the camber to assure that it has maintained its arc while under that tension. With that same tension, look down the stick from the frog end to determine if the bow is straight. There should be no deviation from true.

The flexibility of bow sticks can vary greatly from one bow to another. Here, a matter of personal choice is the primary deciding factor. Softer sticks tend to be more yielding to pressure and, consequently, result in a generally gentler response. A stiffer stick will respond with a crisper, more aggressive sound.

Stick Shape: Bow sticks are either octagonal or round. Round sticks are octagonal at the frog but then become round shortly after the frog. Octagonal sticks tend to be firmer than round sticks. As stated earlier, stiffer bows are generally a bit more responsive than round, more flexible sticks, which tend to produce a gentler response. The choice is up to the player; however, unless a particularly strong opinion in one direction or the other is the player's intention for that particular bow, it is best to strike a midpoint in the choice.

The Choice: In view of all of the considerations listed, the most practical choice of bow for a school string program is a fiberglass bow with horsehair. These bows are inexpensive, well-balanced, very durable, and reliably consistent. Fiberglass bows are available for all string instruments. Should the budget allow for an upgrade in bows, the next choice would be carbon fiber with horsehair. Also durable, these bows are made in various levels of refinement to the point where one can cost close to a thousand dollars. Even if the budget allowed for such a purchase, it would be impractical to have such a bow for almost any school inventory unless the level of achievement warrants it. A good pernambuco or other high-quality wooden bow is also an excellent companion to a good instrument for advanced players, since the bow is a very important part of a string instrument outfit. If wooden or high-end carbon fiber bows are used, they should be matched with compatible instruments and the assigned bow should remain a part of that outfit.

The Frog: The frog is the only part of the bow that moves. Check the fit of the frog by holding the stick with one hand and trying to move the frog from side to side. It should not move in that way. When turning the screw at the end of the bow, the frog should slide back and forth easily while remaining firmly on the stick. On the back of a frog there may be a strip of metal leading up to the bow stick. This strip is called a lining. If the strip is present, the frog is fully lined; if not present, it is half lined. The difference is of little relevance and should not be a major consideration in bow selection.

Balance: Bow balance and weight rank high in the "consistency of inconsistency" category of opinions and arguments in the music world. The weight of a bow, usually measured in grams, can vary as much as fifteen grams within the same instrument category. The average weight of a violin bow is around sixty grams, with the viola, cello, and double bass increasing from that sixty-gram weight in gram increments.

There is no correct numerical weight for a particular bow. The correct weight is what is comfortable and responsive for the individual testing it. The same is the case for balance. Hold the bow under consideration horizontal to the floor with proper hand position and with no instrument. First bounce the bow in midair, and then move it in every direction, duplicating all possible playing motions. Repeat that action with several other bows in order to establish a baseline for the feel. There will be distinct differences in the feel of each bow. Then play the same brief passage with each of those same bows. One will be outstanding. Buy it.

Summary: The bow is as important a part of an instrument outfit as is the instrument itself. Bow selection, often given short shrift, should take place after the instrument is selected and with that instrument present for testing. Decide on a price range, the level of the player, the quality of the instrument for which the bow is intended, and the type of stick desired. For beginners, a fiberglass bow with horsehair is usually the first choice by most teachers because of its strength, durability, consistent weight, camber, and balance. If that is the choice, there is little need to go through the testing process because with very few exceptions, fiberglass bows made by the same manufacturer are reliably similar.

When selecting other than fiberglass bows, a trial procedure is essential, with the bottom line being how it sounds to the ear of the player and how it feels as it is being used to make those sounds. Having the opinion of a listener who is not playing will also aid in the decision-making process, but it is the player who should make the final decision. Softer, more flexible sticks will make smoother, warmer sounds, while stronger, less flexible sticks will produce a brighter, more aggressive sound. The choice is personal.

Chapter Fifteen

Buying Brass Instruments

Brass instruments are mechanically very similar. They all use a cup mouthpiece, have tubing that is adjustable to some degree, and have valves to change the open tones. Although they are called brass instruments, some of them are made of other metals, plastic, and alloys. The one exception to having valves is the slide trombone, which has a slide in place of the valves. However, there is also a trombone that uses valves as do all the other brass instruments. Just for the record, the official name for these instruments is *labrosone* (lip reed), part of the aerophone (wind) category of instruments.

A process that can be used for selecting a brass instrument could rise to a degree of sophistication that ultimately becomes self-defeating. One of the most important concerns when one selects any wind instrument is intonation. The structural design that is necessary for valve brass instruments to function results in inherent intonation problems. One will find extended dissertations on how a player can deal with these through the use of embouchure adjustments. Many brass instruments have built-in triggers, slide adjustments, and other structural modifications to ameliorate the problem. These functions help, but the problems still remain.

When selecting brass instruments for a school program, the question arises concerning the degree to which the buyer should pursue the issue of inherent intonation problems. The answer is to the degree that will satisfy the needs of the intended students. Once again, the issue of supplying them with the best possible equipment is paramount, but, so is the issue of the budget. How to proceed? Start by avoiding off-brand instruments that have no track record. Some may be acceptable but even if they are, there is a danger of inconsistency. The best bet is to stick with those manufacturers who have been making instruments for decades. If anyone has come close to solving the problem, it is they. The parts of the instruments to be checked are as follows.

Valves: The two kinds of valves used on brass instruments are piston and rotary. The finishes used on valves are nickel-plating, stainless steel, and Monel, a nickel-copper alloy that performs smoothly and is less inclined to corrode than nickel-plate. Most student instruments have nickel-plated valves, upgraded instruments will have Monel-plated valves, and professional-grade instruments, stainless steel, or Monel-plated valves. It is imperative that the valves function smoothly, respond quickly, and are fitted to close-enough tolerances so as to not allow any air leakage. Student instruments are generally built with slightly looser tolerances, while professional-grade instruments have closer tolerances.

Valve Springs: Many valves are fitted with a spring that returns the valve to its original position after being depressed. Three possible configurations for springs are an around-the-valve stem system, encased in a cylinder between the stem and the valve body (these are called boxed springs), and under the piston within the valve casing held by the bottom valve cap. The boxed-spring configuration is preferred by some for student use because it is enclosed and less vulnerable to well-intended but inexperienced handling.

Slides: Brass instruments are replete with slides. They are used for tuning and cleaning the instruments and, on the trombone, for note articulation. All slides must fit securely if there are to be no air leaks. Slides also need to move easily and smoothly. Two possible construction issues that can cause a problem are slides that are too tightly fitted in an effort to avoid leaks, and the converse, where in an effort make them move easily, they are too loose and not airtight. Avoid both extremes by insisting on firm but free-moving slides.

Water Keys: Water keys (spit valves) are devices used to drain condensation from the tubing on brass instruments. The three types are the swing arm, Amado, and Saturn water keys. The swing arm is the most common, consisting of a spring-loaded key with a spatula on one end and a cork or rubber stopper on the other end. The cork or rubber stopper covers a collar that surrounds a hole from which the condensation drains. Press the spatula, the key opens, and the condensation drains. A small but significant refinement on this device is a rubber stopper with a nipple that fits into the drain hole when the key is closed. The purpose of that nipple is to fill in the distance from the stopper to the inside of the slide and thereby erase any turbulence that may occur when that space exists.

The Amado-type water key has a spring-loaded piston contained within a housing unit soldered directly over the drain hole. Press the button on the side, a valve opens, and the fluid drains. This unit works well provided it is properly maintained. If it is not lubricated and kept clean, it can stick in either an open or shut position. Because of this maintenance requirement, the

Amado key may not be the best idea for school-owned instruments to be used by young students.

The Saturn water key works on the principle of the Amado but uses a ball bearing in place of the piston. In so doing, the likelihood of a jammed mechanism is lessened. Press the ring on the side of the key, and the fluid drains. This may be the best choice for student and school use.

Braces: The tubing on all brass instruments is held together and supported by braces that are soldered onto the instrument in appropriate places. Each manufacturer has its own design and location for these braces. Buyers of school-owned instruments need to evaluate the durability and method of the installation of the braces on any instrument being considered for purchase.

Weight: The weight of a brass instrument is an overt manifestation of its construction and durability. Heavier instruments are made with thicker metal. The question arises as to whether this is a plus or a minus. Where durability is concerned, it is more likely for an instrument made of a heavier-gauge metal to bounce when dropped, a distinct advantage when dealing with young children in a school situation. In contrast, a heavier instrument will be more difficult for a young child to hold and manipulate. Additionally, there is the issue of sound production, since the density of tubing and bell on a brass instrument is directly connected with the instrument's tone quality.

Instruments constructed with lighter-weight metal tend to produce a brighter sound, whereas instruments built with a denser, heavier metal will tend to produce a darker sound. A careful evaluation of the intended use of the instruments under consideration is recommended. Give serious thought to the importance of durability versus tone quality, along with the need for the player's physical comfort.

Balance: Balance is a consideration especially for the brass instruments that are held parallel to the floor while being played. The trumpet, cornet, flugelhorn, trombone, and French horn all fall into this category. If the instrument is heavy, a young player will have the tendency to let the instrument gradually drop away from the lips and, in so doing, will affect the embouchure. Once again, the buyer must exercise judgment in deciding priorities.

Bell: All bells on similar instruments tend to look much the same; however, they can be constructed of either one or two pieces of material. A one-piece bell, by virtue of the consistency of the sheet of metal, tends to vibrate more freely. That characteristic, in conjunction with the flare of the bell, will determine the tone quality of the instrument. The choice is in the "ear" of the beholder.

The material used to make a bell will also affect its sound. Yellow brass with a high copper content will produce a brighter sound than gold brass, which will be heavier, and produce the darker sound. Pure silver bells are available at a cost that is not usually within a school budget. Should silver bells be a consideration, they will generally produce a fuller, rounder sound by virtue of silver's greater inclination to amplify the upper partials of a pitch.

Bore: The bore (inner space of the tubing) plays an important role in determining the tone quality and playing resistance of a brass instrument. Instruments are usually offered with a choice of several bore sizes indicated by the terms *small*, *medium*, and *large*. These classifications refer to the internal dimension of the tubing of the three valve slides and are measured in millimeters.

The idea that smaller produces a lighter sound and larger, a bolder sound applies to the bore of brass instruments with a caveat. Although the label the manufacturer gives to the bore size is significant, it is its rate of expansion from the leadpipe to the bell section in conjunction with the diameter of the conical tubing that actually play a role in the final tone quality of an instrument. A slower expansion or taper creates greater resistance, whereas a faster expansion creates less resistance. A smaller bell size will produce a brighter, more aggressive sound, whereas a larger bell will result in a mellower sound. Finding the correct balance of leadpipe to bell size with a compatible bore size that will serve the need of a student population is the challenge of the buyer.

An additional consideration for a buyer of instruments for young players is that larger-bore instruments require greater lung capacity and breath control. If this might be an issue with the general population for which the instruments are being purchased, the buyer might consider leaning toward medium to small bore sizes.

Mouthpiece: Every newly purchased instrument will come with a mouthpiece the manufacturer believes appropriate for that instrument. Unfortunately, those mouthpieces may not be appropriate for the player. It is recommended that the school inventory include a variety of different-size brass-instrument mouthpieces that students can use to help determine the size that will be most effective for their use. Since the size, shape, and structure of embouchures differ, the teacher must invest the time needed to make a prudent selection of the mouthpiece. The following general principles of brass-mouthpiece construction will help in the mouthpiece-selection process.

1. Because each player has a unique dental and lip structure that creates a unique embouchure, it follows that a suitable mouthpiece must be selected on an individual basis in order to achieve the best possible results.
2. Each instrument must have a mouthpiece that matches the design dimensions of that particular instrument, especially in relation to the size of the instrument's leadpipe.

3. The mouthpiece's inner dimensions are critical to its output and must be matched with the player's needs and the leadpipe of the instrument.
4. Mouthpiece model numbers and letters indicate the size of the various parts of the mouthpiece. Low numbers indicate larger cup diameters. High numbers indicate smaller cup diameters. Models without letters following the numbers have medium-deep cups, producing a full, rich, deep sound. Models with letters following the number are sized as follows: "A" cups are very deep; "B" cups are medium deep; "C," medium shallow; "D," shallow; "E," extremely shallow; and "W" models have a wide-cushion rim for thick, soft lips.

When selecting a mouthpiece, evaluate the player's physiological characteristics in relation to the instrument mouthpiece's size requirements. A French horn mouthpiece is considerably smaller than that of a tuba. Then determine what combination of mouthpiece components will serve the player best. It is essential that the player try a number of mouthpieces that approximate the proportions that have been decided on as appropriate. In the final analysis, the response of the mouthpiece to the player's embouchure should determine the choice.

The Anatomy of a Mouthpiece: All brass mouthpieces consist of six components—the rim; cup; shoulder; throat; backbore; and shank. The factor that distinguishes them from one another for the different instruments is the size of their components and, therefore, the overall size of the mouthpiece. The design of a tuba mouthpiece is similar to that of all other brass mouthpieces, but it is sized to fill the acoustical requirements of the instrument. The effectiveness of a mouthpiece is the result of the combination of its components in conjunction with the player's lips or embouchure. The totality of these factors ultimately becomes the sound generator.

The Mouthpiece Rim: The rim of a mouthpiece is the outer edge that comes into contact with the player's lips. The size and shape of the rim are generally described as being wide, narrow, round, or sharp. When selecting a mouthpiece, one should consider the shape of the rim in relation to the player's lips. Since the rim size and shape profoundly affect the player's tone quality and endurance, it is important to select a rim that is best suited to the player's lip shape and size. The most effective width of the rim for an individual is usually similar to the lip size. Most players will need a medium rim. Players with thick lips would most likely benefit from using a wide rim, while players with thin lips should use a narrow rim. Although a reasonable degree of comfort is desirable, priority must be given to the sound-generation response that the player will derive from the rim selected. The size and shape of the rim that produces the best sound, not the one that feels best, should be the one chosen.

The Mouthpiece Cup: In the structure of the mouthpiece, the rim is followed by the cup. The factors to consider in choosing the cup are its diameter and depth. The diameter provides the area in which the player's lips vibrate, so a diameter that is too small might restrict the vibration. Using the widest diameter possible will allow the player's lips more vibrating space and thereby permit a fuller sound.

The depth of a cup follows the principle of acoustics that permeates all of musical-instrument design. The larger the instrument, the deeper and more mellow the sound. Deeper cups favor lower sounds, whereas shallower cups favor higher sounds.

The Shoulder: The shoulder of a mouthpiece is the door to the throat. The shoulder controls the flow of air into the throat of the mouthpiece and, in so doing, greatly affects the tone quality. Again, selection must be predicated on the embouchure of the player. The size that allows the player to produce the best sound with the least effort would be the one of choice.

The Throat: The throat of the mouthpiece also follows the general acoustical principle of size-to-pitch relationship, that is, larger instruments favor lower sounds and vice versa. It is therefore necessary for the player to choose a mouthpiece throat size that will best serve the other components selected for the mouthpiece in question. When one chooses a mouthpiece, remember that since the throat controls the airflow, too small a size will tend to smother or mute the extreme registers, while too large an opening will not provide sufficient control for the optimum tone.

The Backbore: The backbore of the brass mouthpiece is the column that follows the throat. This portion of the mouthpiece is not generally considered in terms of its size but rather in terms of its shape. The backbore starts out at the throat at its (the backbore's) narrowest and then enlarges as it reaches the end of the shank. To repeat, larger spaces produce deeper and louder sounds, while narrower or smaller spaces restrict the flow of air, offering more resistance and favoring higher sounds.

The Shank: The shank of the mouthpiece is the portion that enters the mouthpipe of the instrument. It is essential that the shank make perfect contact with the inside of the mouthpipe in order to avoid a leak or space that would cause turbulence in the flow of the vibrating air column.

Material: Another consideration in evaluating brass mouthpieces is the materials from which they are made and the effects those materials have on tone production and playing ease. Sterling silver, German nickel silver, silver or gold-plated brass, plastic, Lucite, aluminum, and stainless steel are the materials most commonly used. There are as many opinions as there are players about which is best, but sterling silver, silver plate, and nickel plate are by far the most popular.

One additional option available in the selection of mouthpieces for brass instruments is the detachable rim that screws on and can be used with mouthpieces of various components. With a screw-on rim, a player can switch mouthpieces when doubling on an instrument other than the player's usual instrument and not have to adjust to a different rim. The screw-on rim also allows the player to switch to a Lucite rim when playing outdoors in cold weather. This is particularly convenient, since the player can avoid using a metal rim that can freeze onto the lips.

The number of possible combinations of mouthpiece components can be expressed mathematically as seven factorial, since seven different parts can be combined. This means (multiplying $7 \cdot 6 \cdot 5 \cdot 4 \cdot 3 \cdot 2 \cdot 1$) that there are 5,040 possible combinations of mouthpiece components. Good luck!

Finish: All brass instruments must have a finishing coat to keep the raw brass from tarnishing. At least that was the prevailing wisdom until some players theorized that the finishes interfered with the resonance of the metal and decided it would be best to play an instrument with no finish. Not so, proved Renold Schilke, president of the Schilke Brass Instrument Manufacturing Company. Schilke selected three identical trumpets. He finished one in lacquer, the second in silver plate, and the third left unfinished, and presented them to a series of professional trumpet players to evaluate. The result was that the silver-plated and raw brass played the same, whereas the lacquered brass was significantly different. The lacquer on the bell of the instrument had actually doubled the thickness of the bell and thereby changed its resonating ability.

Given that bit of information, what is the buyer of brass instrument for school use do? Unless the search for an instrument is being conducted for a professional player, the previous may be a bit more information than one needs to know. School budgets rarely allow for the purchase of silver- or gold-plated instruments, and if they do, perhaps it would be better to use those extra funds to buy more equipment. One should resort to pragmatism and go with the lacquer.

Chapter Sixteen

Buying Woodwind Instruments

Note: Although woodwind instruments are often made of wood, they can also be made of brass, metal alloys such as nickel silver, or substances such as plastic, sterling silver, or gold. They are given the woodwind name because of the wooden reed that is used to play many of them. An exception would be flutes, most of which are made of metal. There are some wooden flutes but those are not commonly used. One of the many wonders of the music world!

The Process: Choosing woodwind instruments to purchase for school use is very challenging, even for a woodwind major. All woodwind players know at the very onset that these instruments have inherent intonation problems. Finding some with the fewest intonation problems is the best that one can expect. One of the causes of these problems is the tone generator, that is, the mouthpiece/reed/ligature setup. Therefore, it is essential that the person who is to test woodwind instruments begin with a mouthpiece/reed/ligature combination that, in the player's estimation, has been tested on a known instrument and deemed to be the best possible setup. After achieving a positive result, the tester should use that same arrangement to test similar instruments. Be sure to warm up the instrument to be tested before making judgments.

There are many highly sophisticated, worthwhile tests that a professional can apply to a high-end instrument. Those tests are fine when searching for a particular intermediate- or professional-level instrument. A teacher shopping for a quantity and variety of student-level instruments must, through necessity, modify the procedure to fit the circumstances. The goal should be to weed out the worst offenders while selecting a set of instruments that will perform for the students with reasonable effectiveness.

Following are some hints for teachers who are charged with the responsibility to select, evaluate, and purchase a variety of woodwind instruments for a school program. These suggestions are not intended to be the last word on the subject. A complete evaluation of any single instrument is a complicated task requiring a highly skilled, experienced professional who is a specialist in the instrument in question. As is the case with all things musical, opinions on how one should go about the task of testing an instrument vary greatly.

A valid testing protocol should start with an established format that includes various short musical examples chosen to best challenge the instrument. Among the passages should be diatonic and chromatic scales and short musical passages requiring tonguing, slurring, and any articulation patterns appropriate to the situation. Select or create exercises around notes that are known intonation offenders for the instrument under scrutiny. Follow this by judging the inherently out-of-tune notes individually with an electronic tuning device to determine how far the pitch is off. Next, try to force the offending note into tune with embouchure adjustments. Then decide if that particular instrument is acceptable based on how severe the problem notes are. One will never find perfection. The decision will have to be based on how far from perfection is acceptable.

Tone Quality: Tone quality is a factor to consider when judging an instrument. Again, this is a product of the mouthpiece/reed/ligature arrangement, or in the case of the double-reed instruments, just the reed in conjunction with the embouchure of the player and the instrument. Tone-quality judgment is subjective and individual. If the player hears a tone that resembles what he or she is accustomed to hearing on his or her instrument when using the same mouthpiece/reed/ligature setup, the instrument being tested will probably be acceptable as far as tone quality is concerned.

There is a somewhat esoteric viewpoint that one might want to consider. Sound registers in the human mind as a product of one's physical ability to hear, along with a combination of factors the brain is predisposed to accept as being a good sound. These predispositions develop from a lifetime of hearing a variety of sounds prevalent in a particular musical and social environment. What sounds good to one person may not to another. One learns to expect a certain sound to come from a particular source based on repeated previous exposure to that sound that came from that source. "Good" sound, therefore, is almost totally subjective.

The best way to deal with the challenge of checking a number of student-level instruments is to evaluate the consistency with which the instruments perform as they are played through the registers. The tester should listen for pitch accuracy and tone quality while judging resistance, the ease with which the instrument is performing, its projection, the resonance and openness of the sound, and the facility with which the keys perform.

Key Mechanism: The level of craftsmanship and the quality of the material used in the construction of any instrument is worthy of serious scrutiny. The physics of woodwind instruments dictate that a carefully adjusted, complex key mechanism must be in place for the instruments to function satisfactorily. All woodwind instruments rely on a series of keys and pads to cover tone holes in the body of the instrument. The slightest misalignment of a key or improperly seated pad can render an instrument unplayable. It is therefore essential that the instruments being reviewed have a key system constructed of a metal that is strong enough to withstand the repetitive pressure exerted on it during playing, while maintaining the adjustment required to ensure there will be no air leaks. Add to that the fact that the instruments will be used by inexperienced young people and the likelihood of bent keys is compounded exponentially. The issue here becomes one of selecting instruments that have keys made of a durable material.

Keys for student-level instruments are usually made of nickel silver, also called German silver, a copper alloy containing nickel and at times zinc. This alloy does not contain any silver. The keys on student instruments are usually available in a nickel or silver plate. Nickel plate is usually the key of choice because it is durable, does not tarnish, and is less expensive than silver. There is a small segment of the population that is allergic to nickel-plated keys. In consideration of that possibility, when purchasing numerous instruments for a school program, one might purchase one or two instruments with silver-plated keys for use by those individuals who experience a negative reaction to nickel-plated keys.

Because there are varying degrees of strength in keys regardless of the metals used, it is suggested that the buyer test this strength by exerting slight lateral pressure on the longer keys to judge their flexibility. Not too hard, for they may break. A good, strong key will not flex. Drop-forged nickel silver keys are most common in good student-model instruments because of their strength. The information found in the instrument literature will tell how and of what material the keys are made.

Key systems must be precisely adjusted if they are to function properly. To that end, the systems contain adjustment screws from as few as one on a clarinet's A key to as many as eleven on oboes. These screws facilitate key adjustments to a very close tolerance, so logic would dictate that more are better. There is another side to that dictum in that adjustment screws do go out of adjustment on their own. The more screws there are, the greater the chance for problems to arise. What's a teacher to do? There are less-sophisticated key systems with fewer adjustment screws that limit the chance of those going out of adjustment while limiting the fine-adjustment option. Whatever the choice, one should not try to adjust a complex mechanism of an instrument with more than one or two screws. Leave it to the professionals.

Flutes, and clarinets to a lesser degree, are made with plateau keys. On student-model flutes, this type of arrangement is very common and highly recommended for school use. Flutes with open holes are more expensive and do produce a somewhat better tone than those with plateau keys. Open-hole flutes are more difficult to play for beginners, especially those youngsters with small fingers. Should the budget allow for open-hole flutes, there are plugs that can be used to close the holes, turning them into plateau keys. These can be removed as needed.

Oboes and clarinets are also available with both open-hole and plateau (closed-hole) keys. For younger children, oboes with plateau keys are easier to play, but the plateau-key systems are more difficult to keep in adjustment. Clarinets with plateau keys are less common and usually require a special order to buy. These are made for players with small hands who are not willing to wait in order to grow enough to cover the open holes on a traditional clarinet. Plateau-keyed clarinets are an excellent product for young players; however, weaning them off those instruments as soon as is practical should be the teacher's goal.

Two other considerations when one evaluates a flute are the options of a split E key and the inline or offset G key. It is the opinion of most professionals that the value of a split E key for early student use is not significant enough to warrant much consideration. As to the offset G key, the pro side of the issue is that it is easier for young hands to reach that setup. In contrast to that opinion is the view that after learning on an offset system, it will take the student a bit of adjustment to advance to an open-hole system with an inline G key. Another decision to make for the beleaguered teacher/buyer.

Tenons: A tenon on a woodwind instrument is the end of a section that has been reduced in size to fit into another section of that instrument. Tenons on the end of each of the joining sections of woodwind instruments are subject to a significant amount of stress and wear during the assembly and disassembly of the instrument. It is essential that these parts fit firmly with no air leaks, that the insides close the gap between instrument sections inside the bore totally in order to avoid turbulence, and that the fit is smooth enough to allow easy back-and-forth movement without jamming. Because tenons are exposed when the instrument is disassembled, they are at risk of being chipped, dented, or broken. Some instruments will have a supporting ring about the edge to help prevent this kind of damage. Others have tenon caps to be put in place when the instrument is not in use. If possible, these protective devices would be beneficial to the well-being of school-owned instruments.

Options: Student flutes are made entirely of metal. For the record, there are flutes made of wood, glass, and other materials, but these are not designed for school use. The two most commonly used metals are nickel silver and silver plate. Nickel silver is less expensive and eventually will lose its shine. Silver plate, which costs a bit more, will tarnish but can be polished back to its original silver look.

Student flutes are most commonly built with C as their lowest note. There is an option available that extends that lowest note to low B. This note does not appear often in music and is not usually found in the curriculum of young flute players. Unless there is a particular need, pass on this option and save some money.

Flute and saxophone keys are assembled with a system of rods and pivot screws that are connected to a series of posts. The posts are either soldered directly onto the body of the instrument or are attached to a strip of metal called a rib, which is then soldered onto the body of the instrument. Rib construction provides greater stability to the key system and thereby requires fewer adjustments. In the case of the saxophone, rib construction provides the additional service of reducing vibrations that are in excess of those required to produce the instrument's prescribed timbre. Rib construction is common on a saxophone and, if possible, should be the design choice on a flute.

The size of an instrument's bore, that is, the inner circumference of the body, affects tone quality. In the simplest terms, small bores will offer greater resistance, produce a crisper tone, and play in tune more easily. Conversely, larger bores will create less resistance, produce a darker tone, and can be a bit more difficult to play in tune. Student-level instruments usually have smaller bores.

Instrument pads are touted by all manufacturers as having every conceivable quality that makes theirs the best. When one tests an instrument, it is not possible to accurately judge the quality of the pads without removing some and taking them apart. The most practical step to take in order to learn about the pads on an instrument would be to read the accompanying literature, which should describe the pads. One must follow that reading with a careful inspection to be sure that the pads are properly seated. Playing the instrument will tell the story, for if the pad seating is incorrect, the sound will be stuffy, difficult to produce, or squeaky. Fingering the keys of a woodwind instrument starting from the top down consecutively using a hammering strike on the keys with the fingers should produce a hollow pop for each note. The sound of the pop should get progressively lower. The clearer the pop, the better the seating of the pads.

Springs: Springs on woodwind instruments are either flat, needle-shaped, or simple wires. They can be made of blue steel, stainless steel, white gold, silver, or anything else that will work and appeal to some segment of the market. Usually, needle and flat springs are made of blue steel and tend to be of sufficient strength to do their job. Stainless-steel wire springs can be a bit less dependable, as one can never be sure of their strength. To test the resilience of a wire spring, using a crochet hook, unhook the spring from the key, and from the tip of the spring, gently bend it back and forth. It will demonstrate its strength and resilience by how easily it retains its shape and returns to its point of equilibrium.

Summary: Sometimes making decisions on which direction to take when deciding on what to buy can seem overwhelming. For the average school situation with a teacher who is assigned to purchase a number and variety of instruments, the best first step would be to focus on the major manufacturers who have a lengthy track record of making student-quality instruments. More than likely, they will have been confronted with all the possible problems and issues related to the instruments they make and have sought and probably found the most practical solution to those matters. From there, apply as many of the suggestions offered here to your search as are practical, and be sure to include an option for return of any instrument you may find unacceptable. Take delivery, test the instrument at your leisure, and make any adjustments needed.

Chapter Seventeen

Buying Percussion Instruments

Since anything that produces sound by being hit (e.g., a drum), rubbed (gui-ro), shaken (maraca), blown into (whistle), and more can be classified as a percussion instrument, this section will be limited to the basic drums and timpani that would be found in an elementary or secondary school music classroom. Even with this restriction, the list can be daunting, unless it is further limited to the basic necessities for a school instrumental-music pro-gram. It will exclude instruments used for preschool and the early grades but will include the smaller percussion instruments that are commonly found in the scores of music that would be played at the elementary and secondary levels. Basic drums found in most schools are the snare, bass, tom-tom, and timpani. The snare drum is the primary instrument of the section. Each part of a drum has some effect on the sound produced. The drumhead is the main sound source and should be given primary consideration when making a choice of drum equipment.

Drumhead: Drumheads are made of animal hide or some form of polyes-ter. Animal hide, the original material used since the beginning of human history, is sensitive to changes in ambient temperature and humidity. Warm, humid air will cause the skin to soften and lose its brilliance. The reverse happens with cold, dry air, which shrinks and tightens the skin. In the middle of the twentieth century, a polyester film called Mylar was developed by the DuPont Company; this discovery led to the birth of the plastic drumhead. Whether to buy hide or plastic drumheads for school use is probably the easiest decision a teacher will have to make. Hands down, the answer is plastic due to its stability and the great assortment of versions available.

Plastic heads can be found in single- or double-ply and in various thick-nesses, which are measured in millimeters, or one thousandth of a meter. Single-ply heads are most popular and can be bought in 7-, 7.5-, 10-, and 12-

millimeter thicknesses. The concept common to all things musical that smaller produces higher sounds and larger produces lower sounds applies here, in
that thinner heads produce higher upper partials with a resulting crisper
sound, and thicker heads produce a fuller, warmer sound. The caveat here is
that the single-ply head is thinner and as such, less durable. Double-ply heads
are made with two layers of Mylar that can be the same thickness or of
different thicknesses to produce special effects. For school, double-ply heads
with both plies of the same thickness are probably the best choice.

In addition to the standard single- and double-ply heads, there is a laundry
list of designs intended to produce special effects. Among these are coated
heads, which are sprayed with a variety of translucent or colored coatings to
produce different sounds. One should bear in mind that any addition to the
surface of a drumhead will have the effect of muffling the sound to some
degree. This is not necessarily a negative, and for certain musical effects, it
may be desirable. Should a muffled sound be required for a special effect,
heads are made premuffled or with built-in mufflers. This is achieved by
adding a layer of some substance on top or under the head, or having a two-
layer head with oil between the layers. The variety of options is only limited
by one's imagination.

Drum Shell: The drum shell is the body of the instrument, the amplifier
of the sound being generated by heads, and the hub to which all the parts of
the drum are connected. Because of this central position, the shell you purchase should be the best the budget will allow. As with all products, the
variety of versions is extensive. Drum shells can be made of wood, various
plastics, fiberglass, or metal, with wood being the material of choice for
acoustical reasons, but metal or plastic the material of choice for practical
reasons. Young school children will go through a period in their development
where they may be less than graceful in their movements. A good, tough
instrument that will perform well enough but bounce when dropped may be a
better choice for school use than is a more resonant but more fragile instrument.

Shells are built in different diameters and depths. With reference to
sound, once again, bigger shells produce lower sounds, and smaller shells
produce higher sounds. The most popular snare-drum diameters range from
10 to 14 inches with a possible outside range of 6 to 16 inches for special
effects. The depths of these instruments can range from 3 to 10 inches. A
good choice of a snare drum for general use in a school program would be 14
inches in diameter by 5 inches deep, with a two-ply plastic head.

The remaining parts of a drum are the rim or hoop, lugs, tension rods,
and, in the case of snare drums, a snare. For school use, metal hoops are
sturdy and most practical. The lugs, tension rods, and snares should all be of
a quality commensurate with that of the shell so that choosing these should
not be an issue. The number of lugs can vary on a drum, so consider the fact

that more lugs are more expensive, provide better tension, and will better maintain the drum's tuning, but the drum will be more difficult to tune. Conversely, fewer lugs are easier to tune but can provide less tension stability.

Bass Drum: Bass drums are similar in structure to the snare drum except that bass drums are bigger and have no snare. The largest bass drum is used for concert bands or symphonic orchestras. These drums range in diameter from 32 to 40 inches with an average depth of about 20 inches. This type of bass drum would be best for general use in a school program. The sizes can vary significantly, so selection should depend on the desires and needs of the school program.

Another type of bass drum referred to as a kick drum is used as part of a dance band or trap set of drums. This bass drum is constructed in the same manner as the others, is played with a beater connected to a pedal, and can also vary in size. If a dance band or rock band is part of the program, such a drum might be a consideration for the school's inventory.

A third type of bass drum is used for marching bands. It is lighter in construction, is fitted with a harness or carrying device of some kind, and is used in marching bands. Marching bass drums are also constructed in a similar manner to those described above.

Cymbals: Cymbals are categorized by their size and weight because these two factors affect the quality and strength of the sound they produce. Larger and heavier cymbals produce louder sounds. Thinner cymbals produce a lighter, more sustained sound. The material from which cymbals are made is generally a type of alloy that is flexible enough to be formed into the shape and density required to produce the desired sound. These are referred to as sheet cymbals because they are formed from sheets of metal. Better-quality cymbals are constructed from bell bronze, a hard metal used to make bells, and are forged or hand-hammered. Sheet cymbals are usually adequate for a school program. However, if funds are available, go for the better product.

As is the case with many of the percussion instruments, the numbers of types of cymbals and variations of those types is endless. The two kinds of cymbals that should be included in any school inventory are crash cymbals and a suspended cymbal. Some additional types like hi-hat; ride; sizzle; splash; swish; marching; and finger should be considered only if there is a need for them.

The vast variety of cymbals on the market makes the selection for those that are appropriate for a given school program challenging. Cymbals must be compatible with the equipment with which they are going to be used. It is, therefore, wise to have the selection take place after the drums have been chosen. The primary consideration for school use should be size and thickness. These issues are of particular importance if the program for which the cymbals are to be used will be for young children. Size and thickness equal weight. When selecting crash cymbals, the size of the students for which the cymbals are intended should be a consideration. In the case of the suspended cymbal, weight is not an issue. Thin cymbals are lighter and produce a lighter, more sustained sound, but they are more inclined to crack when subjected to high-volume use. Thicker cymbals are the reverse. They are heavier, stronger, produce a stronger sound, stand up to more aggressive use, and generally will last longer.

When viewed from the side, a cymbal will evidence a gradual and then more sudden elevation in the upper surface. The section from the outer edge to the sudden elevation is called the bow. The center elevation or bulge in the center of the cymbal is called the bell. Its size will determine the amount of overtones the cymbal will produce. The size of the bow determines the cymbal's pitch. The greater the bow, the higher the pitch.

The bow has two strike areas. The section closer to the bell is called the ride area and because of its thickness, it offers a bolder sound. As the bow tapers out to the thinner section called the crash area, the sound becomes richer and more self-sustaining.

If a drum (trap) set is in the budget, the set may include a high-hat and ride cymbal. The cymbals used for these setups share all the characteristics mentioned above and can be judged on that basis. Their design and size should be in keeping with the drums in the set and complement the output of those instruments as opposed to overpowering them.

Timpani: Timpani (timpano in the singular) differ from the drums discussed thus far in that timpani are definite-pitched instruments. They share many of the structural characteristics of the other drums but with a more sophisticated technology. Timpani are built on a copper, brass, or fiberglass shell shaped like a kettle, from which their nickname, kettle drum, is derived. The kettle is fitted into a frame that often has two wheels to facilitate transportation, and a pedal used to make quick adjustments in pitch to the heads.

Timpani Sizes: Timpani are made with bowl sizes ranging from 20 to 32 inches in diameter. Larger bowl timpani produce lower pitches. If the school music program will be playing music that calls for timpani, the buyer should consider including at least two timpani to provide the students with instant access to a greater range of pitches. With two timpani tuned a fifth apart and a pedal spread of a fourth (to be explained below), a timpanist is able to play a chromatic scale.

Different-size timpani exist to provide a range of notes usually from C2, second line below the staff in the bass clef, to D5, a ninth above middle C. The following is a list of the notes to which the different-size timpani can be tuned, and the approximate ascending range of notes that can be produced with the use of the pedal.

- A 30–32-inch kettle can be tuned to C2 and pedaled up to F3.
- A 28–29-inch kettle can be tuned to F3 and pedaled up to D4.
- A 25–26-inch kettle can be tuned to Bb3 and pedaled up to Gb4.
- A 23–24-inch kettle can be tuned to D3 and pedaled up to Bb4.
- A 20–22-inch kettle can be tuned to F4 and pedaled up to D5.

Timpani Pedal: Timpani, as definite-pitched instruments, are used to produce a variety of pitches throughout a performance. To facilitate this process, a pedal mechanism is installed in the instrument, allowing the timpanist to immediately change pitches within certain parameters without having to go through the tension rod tuning process. When the pedal is depressed, cables inside the shell of the drum pull down on the rim to tighten the head. When this tightening occurs, the pitch is raised in a glissando to an interval of approximately a fifth above the fundamental tone. The player can stop the pedal at any point when the desired pitch is reached. The timpani pedal must be properly adjusted in order to hold the position set by the player. To check the pedal action on a timpani, conduct the following test:

With the head properly tuned to the prescribed fundamental tone, depress the pedal toe down to its maximum position and release the foot from the pedal. It should remain in that position. Now depress the heel of the pedal down, stopping it at various points along the way. A properly adjusted pedal should remain at any point in its range without having to be held in place by the player's foot. If the pedal does not remain in place, tighten or loosen the knob on the pedal mechanism until the pedal does remain in place.

Drum Set: A drum set, sometimes referred to as a trap set or drum kit, can vary in size depending on its intended use and one's budget. A three-piece set will consist of a snare drum, bass drum, and floor tom-tom, a ride cymbal, crash cymbal, and a hi-hat cymbal. Cymbals are usually included but not counted in a trap set. This arrangement, with the addition of a throne (stool), is sufficient for beginners to experience playing a set. Adding two side or mounted tom-toms would result in a five-piece set, providing the player greater performance versatility. These additions will require appropriate stands and hardware. All the advice on inspection and selection of drum equipment discussed previously in this chapter will apply to this purchase.

Electronic Drums: With the evolution of the electronic synthesizer, the drum industry has developed a product that can produce a variety of percussion sounds. Pads with a resilient drumhead-like surface contain a sensor that, when struck, sends an electric impulse through a cable or MIDI connection to a sound-producing and sound-amplifying system. The individual pads can be designed and programmed to replicate various types of drum, cymbal, or other percussion sounds. Different-size pads are set up on stands in the same configuration as a trap set so the player can experience the drumming process as he or she would on an acoustic drum set. The extraordinary flexibility of this apparatus allows a student to produce an infinite assortment of sounds, duplicating both tuned and nontuned percussion instruments. The set can be used with full amplification for a realistic ambient percussion sound, or it can be used with earphones for practice with very little sound audible in the surrounding area.

Another advantage to this setup when compared to a traditional acoustic drum set is the ease of portability and storage the electronic drums offer. These devices do have a level of contrived sound that can only be judged acceptable or not by the player and the circumstance in which the set is to be used. Additionally, the feel of the set to the drummer, although closely resembling that of a traditional membranophone, does fall a bit short. But under certain circumstances, this electronic drum system may be a good choice due to its musical and physical versatility.

Summary: The bottom line when buying any percussion equipment has several components. First, be sure the price is right and in line with the market value of similar equipment. Next, try to buy the sturdiest equipment the budget will allow. Finally, after contemplating all these suggestions, keep in mind that the primary purpose of the equipment being purchased is to make music. Be certain the equipment is producing sounds that will complement the ensemble for which it is intended.

The number of instruments that can be considered to be in the percussion category is huge, and each of those individual instruments can have numerous iterations. This can make the selection process daunting and challenging, and, as such, may result in the buyer just settling for whatever is easier to buy. To avoid that pitfall, decide on the budget, set acceptable performance parameters for the instruments that will fall into that budget, determine the physical, musical, intellectual, and emotional profile of the students for which the use of the instruments is intended, try to summarize all that information into the most compact form, and use that information to make the best decision possible.

Drumsticks: Sticks and mallets, although sold separately from the instruments, are actually part of the instrument. Drumsticks are made in a variety of sizes and of hard woods such as oak, hickory, or maple. Aluminum and various forms of plastic, fiberglass, and carbon fiber are also used to make these sticks. The sticks come in such a wide range of sizes, thicknesses, densities, and weights that any effort to categorize them would be futile.

There is a labeling system for drumsticks in the music industry that uses a combination of numbers and letters to identify stick sizes. Unfortunately, this system is far from standardized. Many manufacturers use their own proprietary labeling, which adds to the confusion. This being the case, guidance in stick selection will be offered in the most general sense.

The three most common size markings that enjoy a reasonable degree of accuracy are 7A, which is thin and light, 5A, a bit heavier and the most used for beginners, and 5B, the heaviest of the three, used for big bands and rock music. The feel of a drumstick in a player's hands has a significant effect on the individual's performance; therefore, careful selection of a stick most suited to the player and the music being performed is essential. The three factors to consider in selection are the strength, weight, and density of the stick. Because there are so many variations of these design factors, it is recommended that any purchases for general school use include a variety of sizes and types to keep on hand. This purchase will facilitate easy and prompt access to provide for individual differences without having to wait for a new order to arrive. As students progress, they can experiment with an assortment of stick sizes to arrive at the one most appropriate for each individual and the type of music being performed.

Material: Oak sticks are the heaviest and strongest on account of the density of the wood. The strength will provide durability, strong contact with the strike for the player and the weight to produce a strong sound. Hickory is more commonly used because of its strength and lighter weight. It is believed by some that hickory sticks produce a better percussion sound than other woods or materials. Maple is the lightest wood used for sticks and, therefore, may be best to produce a quick, light, percussive effect. Rosewood is a very dense wood, offering durability and a heavier product. Rosewood is the most expensive wood used for drumsticks. There are numerous synthetic products used to make sticks. These are usually more durable than wood and offer an unlimited variety of ways to satisfy the needs of drummers because of the variety of different "feels" to the sticks.

One additional consideration in selecting a drum stick should be the tip of the stick. Tips are either a continuation of the wood from which the stick is made or are made of nylon added on to the stick. Nylon tips produce a crisp sound and are particularly effective when used on cymbals, whereas wooden tips produce a warmer, more subtle sound. Also available are rubber tips, which can slip over the original tip and are useful for practice when a drum is not available or when little sound is desired.

Brushes: Brushes are used for special effects on snare drums and cymbals. Metal bristles are connected to a rigid wire, which is fed through a hollow handle. The wire has a loop on the end used to pull out of the back of the handle to draw the bristles into the front of the handle. When the loop is pushed into the back of the handle, the bristles fan out of the front and the brushes are ready for use. In this manner, the player can adjust the length, spread, and flexibility of the brushes to achieve different effects, and then collapse the brushes for easy storage. There are brushes that do not collapse. These are not recommended for school use, since they do not store well and are more easily damaged.

Mallets: Mallets are sticks or shafts with a bulbous head attached to one or both ends. The shafts and heads of mallets can be made of a variety of materials. The shaft can be made of different types of wood or plastic or other synthetic material. The head can be made of almost anything from metal to soft, wrapped cotton and can be any degree of hardness depending on the intended use of the mallet.

Bass-drum mallets are often called beaters. Their heads can be made of wood or cotton depending on the degree of hardness required for the music being played. These beaters also come with a double head, that is, a head on each end of the stick. The two heads are usually different sizes and can be of different hardness. Two-headed beaters permit the player to quickly change the quality of the sound by using one head or the other. They can also be used to produce a bass-drum roll when the player holds the beater in the center of the shaft and rapidly rotates the wrist from left to right.

Timpani mallets are constructed in a variety of designs similar to those used for other percussion instruments. The mallets consist of a stick or shaft made of wood or a synthetic product to which a head is attached. The head can be made of almost anything from soft material such as cotton or felt to wood. The choice of the mallets to be used is entirely up to the performer, the requirements of the music to be played, and the wishes of the music director. It is not uncommon for a timpanist to own a large variety of mallets of all strengths, head densities, and different shaft materials in order to be prepared for all possible music requirements.

Selecting sticks and mallets for school use should be preceded by an evaluation of the playing level of the students, the grade level of the music that will be played, the equipment on which the sticks will be used, and any additional anticipated needs of the program. The quality of the sticks and mallets under consideration should be as good as the budget will allow. Keep in mind that sticks are used to beat on things and, as such, are subject to extraordinary wear and tear. Inexpensive sticks may need to be replaced more frequently. It is recommended that an assortment of sticks of different sizes and mallets with different heads be kept in inventory in anticipation of loss or breakage, or to fulfill an unanticipated musical effect.

Summary: A vast array of sound-producing devices are labeled "percussion instruments." Buying them can be as easy as picking out a simple tinkle bell to testing a concert grand piano. How to proceed? As is the case with buying anything, a hierarchy of priorities must be established prior to beginning the search. An immediate-needs budget, projected-needs budget, wish-list budget, and bargain-sale-opportunity budget are categories that should be part of the plan. Notice the emphasis on *budget*, for if there is no money, there will be no buying.

The quality of percussion instruments tends to start at a level lower than other instruments because of their comparatively simple architecture. It is possible to make a drum, cymbal, bell, and so on, to sell at a very low price using very poor-quality material that will sound, to some degree, like the subject instrument. The issue is the quality of sound it will produce and the durability or life span of that instrument. A poorly made oboe will not play at all. A poorly made drum will produce a sound, but not a good one. Nor will a poorly made drum stand up to the beating that drums, by definition, must take. It is, therefore, necessary for the buyer of these instruments to perform a balancing act based on the hierarchy of needs stated above.

It is just not easy to be a really good, well-rounded, conscientious music teacher.

Chapter Eighteen

Renting Instruments

Most instrumental music teachers recommend using rental instruments for beginning and younger students because of the flexibility rental programs allow. A reputable rental service will maintain, repair, exchange, and generally care for the instruments, leaving the student, parent, and teacher free from that burden. The operative word in the above statement is *reputable*. For all of the above to take place smoothly, the service must be operated by experienced, reliable, knowledgeable dealers who have trained technicians onsite and who are intent on making a profit from a job well done, not from bilking the customers. Unfortunately, parents and students are rarely, if ever, qualified to evaluate these services. The job then becomes that of the music teacher. Again, no easy task.

Selecting a Company: Selecting a musical-instrument company to recommend for school use is a multistep process requiring an understanding of the many pitfalls in the market, a basic knowledge of the instruments being sought, and due diligence on the part of the teacher doing the evaluation. Musical instrument rental programs abound throughout the United States. They can be found anywhere from the local mom-and-pop music shops to national franchises on the Internet. The reason for this abundance? It is a good business. Unfortunately, because of the almost universal lack of consumer knowledge, it is often a better business for the rental shop than for the consumers.

At this point it may be useful to review chapter 11, which deals with the dealer/teacher relationship. The teacher, who is more knowledgeable in music matters and the needs of the students than most parents, is the best-equipped person to evaluate a music dealership.

The Evaluation Process: Begin the process by paying an unannounced visit to the dealership location. Ask to speak with the person in charge, preferably the owner, and introduce the scope of the program for which you are seeking service. Ask for an overview of the operation, which should include the lines of merchandise that are regularly kept in stock and the availability of any merchandise the school program uses that is not currently kept by the dealer. Examine the shop facilities, and meet the technicians who are responsible for repairs and maintenance of the instruments from each family of instruments. Try to gauge how extensively the repair benches are equipped, what work is now in progress, and who is doing it. Keep in mind that a dealer's ability to service the instruments of a program is the keynote of the program's success. If the instruments do not function, the student will not be able to play.

Among the other observations to make is an overview of the printed music in stock. Is the type of music that is used in the school there? If not, can the dealer get what is needed? Review the accessories on hand and, again, if the program's needs are not there, can the dealer get them? Does the operation have dealerships from established instrument manufacturers of name-brand instruments?

As to the dealer's service to the school, one would want to know if the service is offered at regularly scheduled times, if the representative or delivery person has a reasonable knowledge of the merchandise being delivered, if an emergency request can be filled, and if the dealership is large enough to supply all the needs for the program.

Because musical instruments are very complex and few people know much about them, a nonprofessional out to acquire an instrument by either rental or purchase is a babe in the woods. The best protection for these individuals has to be the music teacher, who can advise parents on what to rent, what to look for when renting, and where to rent from.

The one caveat when recommending a service is the possibility of the suspicion of collusion between the teacher and the dealer being recommended. It is, therefore, wise for the teacher to list more than one dealer. But then the issue can arise as to which dealer on the list is best. If not handled properly, this can also be dangerous territory for the teacher. One way to deal with directing parents to the best of several dealers is to have the dealers submit a detailed description of their services and circulate that information with the list. The best will most often shine, and the parents will decide and spread the word. It is essential to ensure that the renters will have an option to return, exchange, or replace an instrument within a prescribed time period. This will give the teacher an opportunity to check the instrument to ensure it meets the standards set by the teacher.

A teacher should advise the parents who are renting an instrument directly from a dealer that the instrument and its case should be clean and have no major visible defects. A good-quality professional rental service will present an instrument that is either new, is not new but looks new, or is a least in good playing condition, clean, and properly prepared. After a parent has accepted a rental that has met all of the standards described here, the teacher can then check the instrument for mechanical perfection.

Rental Plans: Rental plans can range from a handshake to a multipage, fine-print contract tying the renter into a plan that will ultimately cost more than the instrument is worth. A teacher's role in this phase of the program would be to advise the parent of the many pitfalls that can be associated with musical-instrument rental programs. Caveat emptor! This phase of the rental process requires no knowledge about instruments. It requires the renter to apply due diligence by acquiring information on all the rental plans available. One must read and understand the contracts for each plan and carefully calculate the costs, not based on the initial charge, for that is often a loss leader, but based on the ongoing cost as the player continues with the rental plan. A concerned teacher will do this in advance of recommending a particular company.

Musical-instrument rental plans can range in time and cost from a simple school-year rental for a one-time fee to every arrangement conceivable. The following is information a teacher can make available to parents who are about to embark on a quest for a good deal on renting an instrument.

Month-to-Month Rental: This plan is not recommended because, although it may appeal to the parent to be able to opt out at any time with as little investment as possible, it is more costly and it also permits the student to opt out of study if he or she has a particularly tough week. Studies show that committing to the rental of an instrument for a year has the effect of committing to study for a year.

Three-Month Starter with Renewal: This is a particularly dangerous program, as it introduces the rental as a loss leader with an introductory period for a small price and then follows that with ballooning costs not easily found in the small print of the contract. If the renter does the math, the ultimate cost over an average student rental period can end up being much more than the value of the instrument.

One-Semester-at-a-Time Rental: If the price is right, this may be acceptable except that, as in the month-to-month rental, the option to quit midyear is open, and the midyear renewal will make the total yearly cost higher. This is usually not the best choice.

School-Year Rental: This is the most common and usually the most equitable plan because (a) the time period coincides with the school program, (b) the student is committed to the program for the school year, (c) the price is usually the best of all the rental time periods, and (d) a reliable company will usually give the summer to follow with no charge if the next school year's payment is made prior to the summer recess. When one uses this plan, be sure it includes a provision for instrument exchanges at any time with no charge for the same-priced instrument or a prorated price for a more expensive one.

Full-Year (Twelve-Month) Rental: This program is best if the student wants to begin study at the end of the school year with the intention of continuing in the following school year. Again, when using this plan, be sure it includes a provision for instrument exchanges at any time with no additional charge for the same-priced or a lesser-priced instrument or a prorated price for a more expensive one.

Rent-to-Own: This program is appealing at first glance until one gets into the weeds of the contract. The question here is, do you want to own the first instrument you get? Students, especially young ones, because of their lack of experience in handling an instrument, usually cause more wear and tear than they will as they progress. Also, there is often some likelihood that the student may want to change instruments, so the possibility of a change should be included in the contract. As a student progresses, he or she may need a better-quality instrument. Does the contract allow for upgrades? If so, at what cost?

The major issue in the rent-to-own program is the true value of the instrument and its ultimate cost to the consumer over the rental period. These programs often lack specificity in stating the true value of the instrument in question. The advertising will focus on the low monthly payments with little or no reference to the total cost by the end of the contract. Additionally, and most important, is the total price being charged for the instrument. In many cases, it is the full list price. Keep in mind the fact that it is easy to obtain a least a 30–40 percent discount on the purchase of any instrument online or even in a local music store. In some cases that discounted price can be paid over time or at least put on a credit card that the consumer can pay over a convenient period of time.

Renting an Upgraded Instrument: The rental of a better-than-beginner-quality instrument is often sought by advancing students. A rental program should allow for this change at any time with a differential cost to the consumer. One should seek guidance from a professional on the brand and model of instrument to rent. It is unreasonable to expect a rental service to provide upgraded instruments at the same price as beginner instruments; however, the higher price should be proportionate to the higher value of the upgrade. In the case of stringed instruments where brand names are not necessarily a consistent indicator of a particular quality, one should seek the advice of a teacher or other professional in the decision-making process.

In summary, one must evaluate the quality of the instrument being provided and the entire final cost to the consumer. Will it reflect some kind of reasonable discount, or will it end up being full list price or greater? Consider the fact that the dealer will have to wait a period of time for full payment and so is entitled to a reasonable profit margin, but there should also be some form of discount built into the program that will benefit the consumer.

Renting a New Instrument: Some parents and students prefer to rent a new instrument. Expect to do this at a higher cost than that charged for the traditional used-instrument program. The cost and the rental program will vary depending on the dealer, the quality of the instrument, and its retail value. Renting a new instrument for a beginning student should be necessary only if there are no used instruments available. A reliable company with professional standards can easily provide a used instrument for a lower price. In the case of the instruments in the violin family, there is little advantage to renting a new instrument because generally new stringed instruments produce harsher sounds than older ones.

Renting an Old Instrument: Old nonfretted string instruments of good quality are sometimes offered for rental by either an individual shop owner or the more sophisticated larger companies. An old violin of good quality can be a very good aid to learning for an advanced, mature student who is able to maximize the instrument's potential while caring for it properly. The consumer must check the instrument carefully to ascertain the instrument's structural viability and stability.

When the instrument passes a physical inspection, it is then necessary to determine whether it is capable of producing the sound desired by the student. For this process, see chapter 13. One must play the instrument and put it through the paces as described in that chapter. If the player is satisfied with the physical structure and the sound it produces, rent it. Regarding the cost of renting such an instrument, one must understand that the market is wide open for a determination of price by the consumer and the merchant.

Renting a Shopworn Instrument: The term *shopworn* is used to describe an instrument that shows some evidence of wear. It can take the form of scratches, chips, or any other kind of blemish. Assuming the instrument performs as it should, these defects are cosmetic and should have no effect on the instrument's playability. Some companies specialize in such rentals, offering them at significantly lower prices than the more attractive instruments. Providing that the student does not object, such a rental is usually a good deal monetarily.

Additional Charges: Along with the rental plans there can be add-ons such as damage protection, loss protection, and a long list of accessories and learning aids.

Damage Protection: Damage protection is insurance that covers any damage that may occur under *normal use*. The operative words here are *normal use*. Vandalism or deliberate destruction is usually omitted from this coverage, so if the child is inclined to vent frustrations on the instrument, the parent should be prepared to pay for the damage.

The cost of this insurance can vary greatly. It is predicated on the value of the instrument along with whatever the market will bear. The prices can range from $20 for a school year to as much as $20 per month. This is one of several places where an unscrupulous merchant can take advantage of a consumer, so remember to include this cost in your calculation of the total rental cost for the year. It is possible that a higher extra fee may give you pause to seek another dealer.

Loss Protection: This is insurance against loss, but again, there are caveats to this kind of coverage. One cannot just claim that an instrument is lost and expect to get it replaced. Usually the coverage is effective only in certain locations such as the school, at home, from a car, or under certain conditions such as fire or burglary. A police report and a statement from the principal of the school from which the instrument has been stolen, along with other documentation, are usually required to process a claim.

The cost of this insurance can also vary greatly. It, too, is predicated on the value of the instrument along with whatever the market will bear. Like the damage protection, the prices can range from $20 for a school year to as much as $20 per month. This is another of several places where an unscrupulous merchant can take advantage of a consumer, so remember to include this cost in your calculation of the total rental cost for the year. It is possible that the loss of a rented instrument is covered under one's homeowner's or valuable items policy, so check with your insurance broker before signing up for this coverage with the music dealer. If this extra cost is excessive, you may want to consider seeking another dealer.

School Delivery Service: One consideration that is of some importance is the procedure for servicing a rental instrument. A full-service company will offer an in-school pickup and delivery service where permitted by the school district. The advantage of this program is that the consumer will call the company for the service. The company will assign a pickup day and specific location in the school to leave the instrument. It will be picked up and returned to that place within a reasonable time or sometimes replaced with another instrument. If the rental company is local, there may be a location where the renter can bring the instrument in for prompter service.

Summary: Much thought and research should precede the rental of an instrument if the renter expects to end up on the winning end of this procedure. Renter, beware! What can appear to be an expense of a few dollars a month can, over time (and the study of a musical instrument is over time), end up costing hundreds if not thousands of dollars more than would be necessary if the consumer is prudent in the initial steps.

Chapter Nineteen

String Instrument Care

Unlike many of the items one uses in daily life, musical instruments require a very specific regimen of care if they are to function properly and have a long life. This chapter will outline the processes needed to maintain student-level string instruments in a school situation.

All instruments of the violin family must be thought of as being structurally dynamic because they are made almost entirely of wood held together with temperature-sensitive, water-based glue. Because wood is hygroscopic (readily takes up and retains water), its cellular structure provides a natural repository for moisture, making instruments made of wood an excellent reactor to both the negative and positive effects of moisture. These instruments physically respond to the environment in which they live.

Since string instruments have the capacity to absorb or release moisture, it is essential for their well-being that they live in a climate that is well balanced in both temperature and humidity. If the climate is too dry, the wood dries out and there is a danger of cracking. Conversely, too moist a climate can result in seams and glued joints opening, wood warping, and the formation of mold. Unfortunately, in a school storage situation, the teacher has little or no control of these ambient factors. In most situations the temperature of a school building will not enter the extreme areas. Humidity can be controlled with dehumidifiers and the lack of humidity with humidifiers. That is about as far as a teacher can be expected to go in an effort to balance those factors.

Should a crack occur or seam open on an instrument, it is important to avoid touching that area. Any deposit of skin oils or perspiration can inhibit the effectiveness of the glue used in the repair process. If a crack occurs in a place where there is a possibility of structural damage to the instrument, because those places are at the soundpost, bass bar, or neck/fingerboard joints, the strings should be loosened and bridge taken down immediately to avoid any further damage. Before removing the bridge, place a soft cloth under the tailpiece to prevent scratching the body.

Another possible reaction to extremes in climate can be the raising or lowering of the top of an instrument with the bridge and strings responding likewise. This is especially common in cellos and in the double bass. Moisture during a summer season can raise the top, and drying out caused by winter central heating can lower the top. In such cases, the owner of an instrument that responds in this manner can have several bridges of different heights on hand to accommodate those changes. An alternative to the several bridges for a cello or double bass is an adjustable bridge that can be raised or lowered by turning a screw installed on each leg.

In summary, an owner of a violin, viola, cello, or double bass must be cognizant of the fact that the various woods from which these instruments are made respond to changes in temperature and humidity by expanding and contracting with different degrees of intensity. This dynamic can often result in open seams, cracking, which can occur anywhere, warping of the neck and fingerboard, slipping pegs, and various small parts becoming loose as the glue dries out. Should any of these occur, there is no need for alarm. If properly dealt with, none of these events will significantly affect the performance or value of the instrument. They are just part of the process of living with an instrument made of wood. The possibility of this happening should be given consideration when one plans a maintenance schedule.

The Process: String-instrument maintenance falls into several categories. These are storage, cleaning, and minor adjustments. Major repairs should be left to the professionals.

Storage: When not in use, a string instrument should always be kept in a case, stored in an environment that is comfortable for a human being, that is, not too hot, too cold, too dry, or too humid. Extreme temperature and humidity can cause damage as described above. If instruments are taken from home to school, students should be instructed in the storage process. In transit, the same rules apply. Keep the instrument in the same location you occupy when traveling. Neither the trunk of a car nor the luggage compartment of a bus or plane are acceptable places for storage in travel. Keep the instrument as close as possible to the temperature in which you reside. Instruments used on a regular basis are best kept in tune while in storage. If they are to be stored for an extended period of time, loosen the strings to about a fifth below pitch so the instruments will maintain their setup but not bear the pressure of full tuning. Store them in a place that would be comfortable for human habitation.

Cleaning: After each use, have the students wipe the surfaces of the instrument and the strings with a soft cotton cloth to remove any rosin dust, natural skin oils, and perspiration. These will accumulate and, if left to permeate the surface of the instrument, will cause damage that could affect the sound and diminish the instrument's value. Use a separate cloth for each process to avoid getting rosin from the strings on the instrument and instrument polish on the strings. Violin-family instruments are sensitive to any treatment that may affect the molecular structure of the wood. A good instrument is finished with either spirit- or oil-based varnish. Student-level instruments are often finished in a lacquer spray. The decision concerning what to use to clean and maintain these instruments is therefore dependent on the type of finish. One will find numerous polishes on the market, each touting its own benefits, whether they are real or contrived. Inexpensive instruments finished with a coat of sprayed-on lacquer can be cleaned with any good-quality furniture polish without serious consequences. Higher-end instruments might be better served with one of the commercial instrument cleaners specifically designed for musical instruments. The teacher should arrange for periodic cleaning in order to maintain the instruments' finish and protect them from rosin buildup and general dirt accumulation.

Minor Adjustments: Nonfretted instruments need constant minor adjustments. It is the nature of the beast. The primary ongoing adjustment is tuning.

Adjusting the Bridge: As strings are tuned, they gradually pull the bridge toward the fingerboard in small, almost unnoticeable increments. An occasional adjustment by the teacher will prevent the bridge from falling or warping. After tuning, do a quick check of the bridge, viewing it from the tailpiece side to be sure that the feet are in total contact with the top of the instrument. Also, as stated in chapter 13, check on the side angle view to see if the side facing the tailpiece is at a perfect 90-degree angle from the top of the instrument and that the fingerboard side of the bridge is graduated to a smaller thickness toward its top.

Bridge Placement: The placement of the bridge on the body of an instrument is crucial to obtaining optimum sound production. There are two directions to check. Note the small notches that are cut into the center area of each side of the f hole. Those notches are an indicator of the optimum bridge position between the fingerboard and tailpiece for the instrument. There can be some latitude in that placement if an experienced luthier determines that another position can produce a better sound.

The feet of the bridge should be cut to perfectly fit the contour of the top of the instrument. The feet must then be placed so that looking from the tailpiece, the left foot stands over the bass bar while the right foot stands slightly behind (toward the fingerboard side) the soundpost. In this position, the right foot of the bridge conducts the higher tones to the top of the instrument and down to the soundpost, and this then carries the sound to the back of the instrument. The left foot conducts the lower tones to the bass bar, which transverses lengthwise along the instrument and distributes the sound across the top.

Bridge Dimensions: Since the bridge plays a dominant role in transferring the sound from the string to the body of the instrument, the design and material used to make the bridge, how it is cut to fit the instrument, and its placement on the instrument must be calculated to fill its function in the best possible way. The dimensions for string-instrument bridges are unique to each instrument. Although there are some guidelines for the initial cutting of the bridge, the final product must be cut to fit the contour of the top of each individual instrument and to provide sufficient but not excessive height for the strings to clear the fingerboard.

The height of a bridge determines the distance it will elevate the strings above the end of the fingerboard at two points—the highest- and lowest-pitched strings. The two intermediate strings are set proportionately, and they follow the contour of the end of the fingerboard. If the strings are proportionately set, the player will be able to bow each string comfortably without inadvertently bowing two strings simultaneously. Close attention must also be paid to the spacing of the strings across the top of the bridge so they will span evenly over the fingerboard, starting from the nut and extending over the bridge to the tailpiece. Table 19.1 offers recommended dimensions for fitting bridges.

Table 19.1.

	Height	Thickness	String Spacing
Violin	E 1/8" G 3/16"	1/16"	7/16"
Viola	A 3/16" C 1/4"	1/16"	7/16"
Cello	A 1/4" C 5/16"	3/32"	5/8"
Bass	G 7/16" E 11/16"	3/16"	1 1/8"

Bridge Inserts: The most common material used for bridges is hard maple. It is essential that the wood be hard because it must withstand the pressure and friction of the taut strings. Sometimes inserts of even harder material are used, especially at the point on the bridge where the violin E string makes contact, in order to withstand the cutting action of that very thin taut string. To help prevent wear, ebony, cowhide, rubber, or plastic are used as inserts at the point on the bridge where the string makes contact.

Climate Variations: An issue with bridge height sometimes occurs when the belly or top of an instrument rises or lowers because of a change in the temperature and humidity. This occurs less often in the violin and viola, but more frequently in the cello and double bass. When the climate changes from cold and dry to warm and humid, the wood of stringed instruments reacts by expanding in a hot, humid environment and contracting in a dry, colder environment.

Moisture during a summer season can raise an instrument's top, and drying out caused by winter central heating can lower it. As this expansion and contraction occur and the top of the instruments rises or falls, the height of the bridge in relation to the fingerboard changes. In such cases, the owner of an instrument that responds in this manner can have several bridges of different heights on hand to accommodate for those changes. An alternative to the several bridges for the cello and double bass is an adjustable bridge that can be raised or lowered by turning a screw installed on each leg.

Maintaining Pegs: An ongoing seasonal problem with violins, violas, and cellos is slipping or sticking pegs. As the seasons change, the wooden pegs, which are usually made of ebony or boxwood but can be of other hard woods, expand with the increase in humidity and temperature or contract with cold dry air. The pegbox in which the pegs are installed is usually made of hard maple. This wood follows the same seasonal pattern of expansion and contraction; however, it does so at a different rate from that of the pegs. The result is slipping or sticking pegs. The double bass does not have this problem because of the worm-in-gear mechanism used on that instrument.

Over the past three hundred plus years, the treatment for these problems has taken various forms. Some find applying chalk or soap to the pegs will alleviate the sticking problem. One will find a variety of peg treatments on the market, and they all claim to solve the problem. A liquid product called Peg Drops is most effective in solving the slipping and sticking problem and is convenient to use, since it does not require removing the pegs for application.

A common cause of slipping pegs is improper wrapping of the string around the peg. In this case, wound string buildup at either end of the peg can prevent it from being fully seated in the peg hole. The hole that is drilled in the peg to receive a string should be at the narrow end of the peg. Starting from that point where the string is inserted into the hole, the string should be wound concentrically with the windings aligned firmly against one another as they progress toward the ear end of the peg. If the string is installed in this manner, there is no string buildup and the peg will move easily. A wound string on a peg must not be allowed to build up against the pegbox since this can cause damage to the pegbox and prevent the peg from turning freely.

Fine Tuner: When used over a period of time, the screws on fine tuners will be turned down more than up and will ultimately reach their lowest position, rendering them useless. At that point there is a danger of the under part of the fine tuner coming in contact with the top of the instrument, which severely damages the varnish. It will be necessary for the teacher to regularly check the fine tuners and return them to their highest position before resuming normal use. Should the screws on the fine tuners become difficult to turn, a bit of graphite or any simple dry lubricant will resolve the problem. Use great caution to avoid having any lubricant reach the instrument's finish.

The Tailpiece: The tailpiece should be attached to the end button of an instrument with the tail gut adjusted to the point where the tailpiece reaches the edge of the saddle. The tailpiece should not extend beyond the saddle.

Adjustments: Strings are in continuous contact with the nut, bridge, and tailpiece on an instrument. It is therefore important that some periodic attention be given to those points of contact to ensure that they are wearing properly and are in optimum adjustment to produce the best sound.

The Nut: The nut, which is located directly below the pegbox, controls the distribution of the four strings across the fingerboard as well as the strings' distance or height from the fingerboard. As time passes, it is possible that the glue holding the nut in place will dry out and the nut can become unstable. This is an easy fix since it just has to be glued back in place.

A second and more serious problem occurs when, over time, as the strings are tuned, the slots in the nut that guide the strings will wear down. This causes the strings to be too close to the fingerboard, affecting intonation and causing a buzz. If this situation occurs, it will be necessary to have a professional technician or luthier replace the nut. A small application of graphite (pencil point shavings) in each slot before the strings are installed will ease the friction of the strings on the nut, help reduce wear, and help prevent the problem from happening.

The Bridge: The bridge is the next point of string contact. The previous section discusses bridge placement in detail. As stated previously in the tuning section, when strings are tuned they gradually pull the bridge toward the fingerboard in small, almost-unnoticeable increments. It will be necessary to periodically adjust the bridge slightly back toward the tailpiece to prevent the bridge from warping or falling down.

Bow Care: Bow sticks can be made of pernambuco, brazilwood, fiberglass, or carbon fiber. Wood bows are very sensitive to the atmosphere in which they live and should be kept in the same environment as are the stringed instruments. Advise the students that if a hair breaks while in use, it should not be pulled out of the bow. Ask them to give it to the teacher who will cut the broken hair at the frog and tip with scissors to avoid dislodging the other hairs where they are connected at those two points.

Remind students regularly that when they are finished playing, always loosen the hair to relieve the tension on the stick and on the wedges in the tip and frog that hold the hair in place. After use, remove all rosin dust from the bow stick by wiping it with a soft cloth.

Bow Cleaning: Should the bow hair become soiled or laden with rosin, the hair may be cleaned by wiping it in an up-and-down motion with a soft cloth moistened with isopropyl alcohol. Do not let the alcohol touch the bow stick, because it will damage the finish. After the alcohol has evaporated, comb the hairs so they resume their parallel position and rosin the bow. A kit called The Bow Hair Rejuvenation Kit is available in music stores that contains all that is needed for this process.

Bow Hair Infestation: Dermestids are a species of minute beetles found in animal material such as horsehair. These creatures are sometimes found on the hair of bows that have been improperly stored for a long period of time. Evidence of the presence of these pests would be hair falling off a bow that has not been in use. Should this situation exist, remove the bow from the case, cut off the all the hair with a scissor, discard the hair, and send the bow to a bowmaker for rehairing. Next, vacuum the case thoroughly, giving special care to the corners and edges. Then spray the case with an insecticide, and let the case remain open in a bright, sunlit place for a few days. If there is still evidence of infestation, replace the case.

Summary: Violins, violas, cellos, and double basses require similar procedures and equipment for proper maintenance. A teacher should take the time to develop an understanding of how these instruments react to their environment and to their being handled by children on a long-term basis. Armed with that understanding, maintaining instruments will be a matter of establishing simple routine procedures to be used by the player after each playing session, along with other more elaborate procedures to be carried out by a luthier periodically, as needed.

Chapter Twenty

Woodwind Instrument Care

The Process: Woodwind instruments have a bit more individuality than the instruments of the other choirs. Flutes are made of nickel or silver, clarinets, oboes, and bassoons of wood or plastic, and saxophones of brass. These instruments are built in sections that must be assembled for each use. Therefore, it is important to include in the maintenance program an early lesson on daily instrument handling and emphasize the delicate nature of bridge keys and the frailty of tenons.

Bridge Keys: Bridge keys are a common problem. Bending them during assembly can incapacitate an instrument. Avoiding bending those keys can be easily accomplished with a few simple instructions on correct assembly methods early on in the program. Saxophones that have an octave key that extends beyond the instrument's body to join the neck also fall into this bridge-key category. Some saxophones come with a neck plug to protect that bridge key. The plug should be in place on the instrument at all times when the instrument is not in use.

Tenon: A well-fitted tenon is essential to a well-functioning instrument. Every care should be taken during instrument assembly to ensure that the tenons are not dented or chipped. Students should be made aware of the correct use of cork grease on tenons that need it. The cork grease should be used sparingly and only when necessary. Instruments like the flute and saxophone have metal tenons that need to be clean, perfectly round, and dent-free if they are to function properly. Include in the dialogue the fact that keeping a mouthpiece on a saxophone neck or keeping parts of an instrument together when not in use compresses the cork and can result in a loose fit, needing cork replacement.

General Care: School-owned instruments lack the affection and intimate personal connection a player would normally have with his or her own instrument. School instruments are, in effect, orphans and as such must rely on foster care with the students and teacher as the foster parents. Any well-informed instrument owner who knows the procedure for woodwind care will apply it with reliable consistency to his/her own instrument. In the case of school-owned instruments, the initial daily care must be executed by the students using the instruments while the follow-up, more complex periodic procedures must be administered by the teacher or some other qualified adult.

Wooden Instruments: The woodwind instruments that are actually made of wood (flutes and saxophones are the exceptions) are subject to those hazards associated with wood's reaction to variations in temperature and humidity. Compounding the problem is the fact that these instruments are exposed to a player's warm, moist breath with all the associated detritus contained therein. If a wooden instrument body is to survive, it is essential that consistent routine care be given to the bore.

An issue often not addressed is that of avoiding eating any foods and especially those containing sugar immediately prior to playing. Accumulation of food particles or airborne sugary vapor will result in sticky pads. Swabbing out the bore of an instrument, wiping off the exterior and keys with a soft cloth, and washing the mouthpiece and reed are all steps that lead to a cleaner bore and pads and a better-functioning instrument.

Swabbing: Students should be responsible for swabbing the bore of an instrument after each playing. A lesson for new students might cover the process starting with disassembling the instrument and slowly drawing a swab of choice through each of the individual parts including the mouthpiece. There are swabs designed to deal with the idiosyncrasies of each instrument. A second step, one that is often omitted, is to dry any pads that may show evidence of excessive moisture. These can be attended to by simply placing a small single layer of a soft, absorbent cloth under the pad and gently closing the key on the cloth. The operative word here is gently, for any rough treatment can result in a pad becoming unseated or ripping. Routine application of cork grease as needed is another job for the student.

Case Use: Keeping an instrument in its case and refraining from putting anything in the case that is not part of the instrument will prevent accidental damage and help insure a long, healthy life. When an instrument with a mouthpiece is put away, the ligature screws should be slightly loosened and the mouthpiece capped.

Bridge Keys: Bridge keys are a common problem. Bending them during assembly can incapacitate an instrument. Avoiding bending those keys can be easily accomplished with a few simple instructions on correct assembly methods. Saxophones that have an octave key that extends beyond the instrument's body to join the neck in assembly also fall into this category. These saxophones come with a neck plug to protect that bridge key. The plug should be in place on the instrument at all times when not in use.

The Use of Oil: The maintenance for all woodwind instruments includes cleaning and treating the wooden body; cleaning out the tone holes; cleaning and lubricating keys; checking and cleaning the pads; cleaning and lubricating the cork tenons; washing and sterilizing the mouthpiece where there is one; and when necessary, regulating the keys. If a wooden instrument is allowed to dry out, the body becomes subject to cracking and chipping, the posts loosen, and it is possible that some change in timbre and intonation will occur. This is especially true of the bassoon and the bass and contrabass clarinet. It is, therefore, essential that the wooden body be treated with oil on an as-needed basis.

The Process: A quick Internet search will reveal numerous opinions, some totally conflicting, on what oils to use and how to use them. The recommended procedure to follow is designed for teachers to use on instruments in a school situation. It is intended not to be the last word on the subject but a basic process that has proven useful for this writer over decades.

The Body:

1. Using a soft bristle brush such as a makeup or shaving brush, brush away all the particles of lint, dust, and other foreign matter that have collected between the keys.
2. Inspect the body to determine if the wood is dry or shows any signs of cracking or checking. If an actual crack exists, bring the instrument to a technician for professional repair. If there are signs of dryness or checking, it is time to oil the wood.
3. The choice of oil is one of those enigmas in the music world that is debated ad infinitum. Suffice it to say the trend is toward vegetable oils (some omit olive oil because it can turn rancid) as opposed to petroleum products. All agree that oiling is essential to the good health of a wooden-bodied woodwind instrument.
4. To prevent the pads from being inadvertently oiled, it is a good idea to slip a bit of plastic wrap under the pad and around each key with a pad. With an appropriate-size artist's paint brush, paint a light coat of oil on the body of the instrument. Be sure to spread the oil between the keys and around the posts.
5. Using a handkerchief threaded through a flute swab and moistened with the oil of choice; spread an even coat of oil throughout the bore and the bell.
6. With a cotton-tipped swab, swab the inside of the tone holes with oil.
7. Allow the oil to soak in overnight, and then wipe off the excess oil, being sure to get in between the keys.

The Keys: Using key oil in a needle oiler, a small bottle with a needle tip sold in music stores, deposit a drop of oil at each key-to-post contact. Wipe and gently buff the key rings and spatulas.

Tenon Corks: Moisten a soft cloth with isopropyl (rubbing) alcohol and wipe the corks on the tenons clean. Apply a thin coat of cork grease.

Mouthpiece: Mouthpieces should be washed thoroughly by scrubbing the interior with a soapy solution using a mouthpiece brush.

Nonwooden Bodies: Although saxophones and most flutes do not have wooden bodies, their metal bodies and those instruments with plastic bodies are subject to the same contamination afforded by the player's breath. It is therefore necessary to treat the bore of these instruments as frequently as those mentioned above but using a different method. There is no need for oil but there is a need to clean and sanitize the bore and the mouthpiece. For these instruments one can use any mild disinfectant as long as it is nontoxic and nonreactive to metals. Sterisol is a popular brand of disinfectant marketed specifically for use with musical instruments. Other disinfectants are available touting various virtues. The teacher should research these products and make a selection based on the circumstances in which the product will be used. Wherever possible, a good scrubbing with soap and water followed by a spray of Sterisol will do wonders. All woodwind key systems require the same treatment. See "The Keys" section above.

Summary: Woodwind instruments contain delicately regulated key systems and are exposed to more assembling and disassembling than other instruments. Their bodies are subject to extreme moisture and temperature changes resulting from the player's breath. This being the case, the processes for taking care of these instruments are both more complicated and more frequently required than those of other instruments. Following the procedures outlined here with religious diligence is necessary to keep a woodwind instrument in good playing condition.

Chapter Twenty-One

Brass Instrument Care

Brass instruments require "per-use" care and periodic care. Per-use care consists of lubricating, cleaning, minor adjusting, condensation removal, and any other action needed to ensure the proper functioning of the instrument as it is being used. Periodic care includes any major action or repair such as complete cleaning of the bore and valve slides, replacing corks, bumpers, felts and other small parts. Keeping a brass instrument properly lubricated before each use and cleaned after each use is essential to the well-being of the instrument and its player. These processes are identical for every brass instrument with the exception of those with rotary valves and trombone slides.

Lubricating: All piston valves should be lubricated as needed, usually before every playing session. To do so, remove the valve from its casing, ensure that there is no extraneous debris on the valve, give it a coat of valve oil of choice, and replace the valve in its original position in the casing. This procedure is used by most professionals and is considered to be the best one to use. For young children using this process, there is the risk of their dropping the valve and damaging it (a serious event), putting the valve in the casing incorrectly, dropping or damaging the spring if it is not attached to the valve, or all of the above. The safer way to oil a valve, although not as effective, is to invert the instrument so that the bottoms of the valves face up leaning to the side slightly off right angle. In that position, place a few drops of oil into the hole in the bottom valve cap while working the valves up and down. At this angle the oil will slide down the sides of the valve casing, not pool in the bottom of the valve, and lubricate it without the risks associated with valve removal. To avoid significant damage and save time at the beginning of each class, the second choice may be the better way to go. Teacher's choice!

Water-Key Care: The three types of water keys (spit valves)—the swing arm, Amado, and Saturn—require regular maintenance. For the swing arm type, there are three steps to be taken. Lubricate the pivot screw with an occasional drop of valve oil. Check the cork or rubber stopper to ensure that it is sealing the collar properly. If not, replace the stopper. Finally, be sure the collar hole is clear, allowing easy egress of the condensation.

The Amado water key has a spring-loaded piston contained within a housing unit. Periodically, place a drop of valve oil on the moving parts where the piston slides into the casing. Work the piston in and out a few times to ensure a smooth movement.

The Saturn water key, which works on the same principle as the Amado key, requires the least care. An occasional drop of oil on the moving parts should keep the key in good condition.

Rotary Valves: Rotary valves present a different challenge. They have a rotor on each side that needs lubrication. The valve itself within the casing must be lubricated, and those rotary valves with a mechanical linkage (the mechanism that connects the lever to the valve rotor) have a third part to lubricate. Beginning with the linkage, while working the valve, place a drop of oil on all moving parts of the linkage. In some cases where the linkage is loose or noisy, using trombone slide cream on the offending moving parts of the linkage may remedy the problem. Turn the instrument over with the valve cap side up, remove the caps, and while working the valves, place a drop of oil on the moving rotor.

To lubricate the rotary valve, depress the valve lever remove the tuning slide, and place a few drops of oil in the two tubes. Replace the tuning slide containing the oil. Turn the instrument right-side-up and work the valve. The reason for not putting the oil directly into the tubes that are directly con-nected to the valve is to avoid the possibility of that oil washing slide grease down into the valve and mucking up the motion.

Slides: All brass instruments have tuning or valve slides, which, if not properly maintained, will become stuck in place, a condition that can be difficult to remedy. Valve slides should be moved in and out on a regular basis to ensure their mobility. When the need arises, remove the slides and wipe them clean with a soft cloth. If there is any oxidation, remove it with a mild brass polish. When the slide is clean, lubricate it with a tuning-slide lubricant of choice. Use only enough lubricant to do the job, because any excess may make its way into the valve, causing a sluggish valve response.

Trombone slide lubricants are available in oil and cream form. Each manufacturer—and there are many—will make every claim imaginable on the virtues of his or her product. Again, teacher's choice. Whichever product you choose, use it sparingly, as a thin coat of lubricant on a well-aligned, dent-free slide is all that is needed. Oil is easier to use than cream because oil can be applied with one hand by squirting the oil from the bottle while the other hand holds the instrument. If slide cream is to be applied evenly, it is necessary to remove the outer slide. Additionally, cream requires frequent applications of water from a spray bottle to keep the lubricating factor active. Oil does not.

Bathing: Brass instruments are entirely waterproof. With the exception of a few felt pads, all parts of a brass instrument can be given a bath with mild soap and warm water. Depending on the condition of the instrument, one can opt to clean only the sections of the instrument that are in immediate contact with the player's breath or clean the entire instrument. If the instrument is reasonably clean and just needs a freshening, clean the mouthpiece, lead pipe, tuning slide, and bell section. This will only require the removal of the tuning slide. If the instrument needs a complete cleaning, it will then be necessary to disassemble it entirely.

The Process: To disassemble any brass instrument, use the following procedure:

1. Spread a clean towel on a flat surface large enough to hold all the individual parts of the instrument.
2. Fill an appropriate-size tub with warm water and gentle dishwashing-type soap. Place a large bath towel on the bottom of the tub to act as a cushion that will prevent the instrument from being scratched.
3. Disassemble the instrument, removing all slides, valves, valve cap bottoms, valve finger buttons, valve cap tops, and valve springs not incased in the valves. Any stuck slides or mouthpieces should not be forced out, since this can damage the instrument. What may appear to be an easy fix is not. Leave stuck components to the professionals.
4. Place all the small loose parts with the exception of the valves in a separate container to soak.
5. Wash the valves individually in the soapy water using a soft-bristle brush. Be sure to pass the brush through the valve ports, but take care not to scratch the surface of the valves. Rinse them and lay them out on the towel.
6. With each slide submerged in the soapy water, proceed to scrub their interiors with a snake brush until they are clean. With a soft wash-cloth, wash the exteriors of the slides, removing any evidence of slide grease.
7. Return to the smaller parts and clean them as needed until they are free of any debris. Valve cap bottoms are particularly prone to collecting detritus. Give them special attention.
8. Submerge the entire stripped body of the instrument into the soapy water, and wash the inside and outside as needed.
9. Remove all instrument parts from the soapy, now not-so-clean water, drain the tub, replace all the parts back in the tub, and refill it with

clean, lukewarm water. Rinse all the parts thoroughly and lay them out on the towel as each one is deemed to be perfectly clean and rinsed. Dry all parts thoroughly with a soft cloth.

10. Grease the slides and replace them. Assemble and oil the valves and replace them with their springs if separate. Replace any felts or corks as needed. Your clean instrument is now ready to go!

Exceptions: The process described above is applicable to almost all brass instruments; however, the trombone and French horn require a slightly different approach to handling their pitch-altering mechanism, that is, the slide on the trombone and the rotary valve mechanism on the French horn.

The alignment of the inner slide on a trombone must be exact to the millimeter if it is to perform properly. When removed from the outer slide, the alignment of the inner slide becomes very vulnerable to misalignment. Great care must be taken to ensure that the two now-unsupported inner slides are kept in a perfectly parallel position and that they are not inadvertently bent out of alignment.

The French horn rotary valve mechanism can take three forms. It can be connected to the key spatulas with a rod-and-screw mechanism, a cotton fiber chord, or with nylon cord. Each must be handled in a different manner if the valves are to be removed to be cleaned. Mechanically connected valves must be disconnected at the point where the connecting rod meets the valve. It is not necessary to disconnect the spring part of the action as long as the valve is free to be removed. The valves can then be removed by unscrewing the valve caps, and the cleaning process can begin.

If the valves are connected by a chord, just unscrew the points of connection and proceed with the valve cleaning. Cotton fiber chords must be replaced with new chords. Nylon chords can be reused. In both cases, it would be best to replace the chords with new nylon if that is convenient.

Summary: The good news about cleaning brass instruments is that the process for all of them is quite similar. Cleaning is a matter of disassembling the instrument, cleaning the parts as needed, drying them, and then lubricating and reassembling those parts. Letting something dry will leave a residue, whereas drying with a cloth will prevent that from happening. Warm water, a gentle soap, a tub of water, and a table to work on are all that are needed. Additionally, almost no parts of these instruments will need any significant adjustments when the cleaning process is done properly. At the very most, it may be necessary to replace the felt or cork valve washers, water-key cork, and possibly the valve bumper corks and strings on an instrument with rotary valves.

Chapter Twenty-Two

Percussion Instrument Care

Percussion instruments by definition are mostly things that are designed to be struck. Because they are sturdy, resilient, and made to take a beating, they are often thought of as not needing much care. Not true! They are the most neglected instruments in a school inventory. Like all instruments, percussion instruments need care if they are to fulfill their roles as musical instruments.

Drums of all kinds are composed of a shell, one or two heads, and various other parts depending on the kind of drum. The shell, which is the body of a drum and the primary support system for the remaining parts, is subject to warping and breaking. The remaining parts that are attached to the shell are actively involved in producing sound. When struck, some parts are in motion and have a variable life span, while others are static and more durable. All must be maintained if they are to live a long and productive life. Regular as-used care and periodic cleaning and maintenance are required for all percussion instruments.

It is not uncommon to walk into a school music room and see any number of percussion instruments standing on the rear riser, uncovered and open to whatever misfortunes can befall them. On an as-used basis, when a session is ended, percussion instruments should be properly packed away and stored in a manner that is in keeping with the school-provided facility. Not only will this protect the instruments from damage, but it will also keep them cleaner and better protected from ambient variations of temperature and humidity. There is a hard-shell case and a soft bag for just about every drum size and shape. Hard cases are preferable, but if they are not in the budget, the soft ones will do. The primary concern is to protect the heads from breakage and the shells from being chipped, scratched, or suffering major damage, all while keeping the instruments clean.

Cleaning: Percussion care includes regular surface cleaning, periodic in-depth cleaning, lubricating, regulating, and tuning. Regular cleaning entails simply wiping the instruments, including drumheads, shells, stands, and cymbals. For a more in-depth cleaning of drums, follow these steps:

1. Release the snare (if the drum has one), and disconnect it from the drum.

2. Using a drum key, remove all the tension screws and remove the rims and heads.

3. For the shell, use a soft, damp cloth to wipe down all the exterior and interior surfaces and then dry with another soft cloth. Do not use any cleaner that contains ammonia.

4. Put a light coat of wax on the shell edges where the heads come in contact with the shell to facilitate the movement of the heads when in place.

5. If desired, a spray polish like Pledge can be used to give a light protective wax coat to the shell's surface.

6. Drumheads can be cleaned with a soft, damp cloth or a liquid window cleaner as long as it is free of ammonia. Use only as much liquid as is necessary to clean the dirt off the heads. Excessive moisture can damage the heads.

7. Metal rims can be cleaned and polished using the same cleaning solution as is used on the heads. For a high shine, an appropriate metal polish can be used.

8. Tension rods collect dirt in the threads. These can be cleaned by spraying a bit of WD-40 on them. Then take a cloth in the palm of the hand, place the threaded part of the rod in the center of the cloth, close the hand with the cloth around the rod, and with the other hand turn the rod in the cloth. A surprising amount of grime will come off on the cloth.

Cleaning Cymbals and Hardware: Cymbals collect dirt and grime because they are grooved, subject to direct contact with the player's hand perspiration and natural skin oils, and are often left in the open without covers. The easy fix is a simple wipe with a damp, soft cloth and if needed, a mild chemical-free detergent. A more ambitious effort would entail polishing the cymbals with a brass polish. Several words of caution! Metal polishes can be messy, so wear gloves, keep the operation away from the other equipment, and be sure to remove all residual polish from the cymbal in the final buffing process. The same process can be applied to any other metal parts on the equipment except that the polish to be used should be appropriate for the metal being treated.

Tuning Drums: Although drums other than the timpani are considered to be instruments of indefinite pitch, in fact there is a tuning process that should be used, and there are pitch considerations for the process. The procedure used to tune a drum is essentially the same for all drums. The tension or tightness of the head will determine the nature of the sound produced. The head is tightened by turning the tension rods in a clockwise direction. To loosen the head, turn the tension rods in a counterclockwise direction.

Adjusting the tension of the heads changes the sound produced and simultaneously changes the feel of the drumsticks as they strike the head. Tighter heads produce crisper, higher-pitched sounds with a more resilient stick rebound. Looser heads produce mellower, lower-pitched sounds with a less resilient stick rebound. The choice is entirely up to the performer and should be determined by the type of selection being played and the venue in which the performance is taking place.

The Process: Tuning a drumhead requires a bit more than just random tightening or loosening of the tension rods. A snare drum is used as an example in the following procedure:

1. Release the snare by flipping the lever on the side of the drum.
2. With the head loose but securely in place and with little but equal tension on the tension rods, depress the center of the head to assure it is firmly seated on the shell. Be sure that all the tension rods are turned into the metal sleeve (called a lug) connected to the drum shell so that an equal amount of each tension rod is visible.
3. Select any tension rod as a starting point. Lightly tap the head with a drum stick about two inches from the rim opposite that tension rod and simultaneously tighten it to the degree where the head begins to show some resistance and the sound begins to change.
4. Repeat the process on the tension rod directly opposite the first one. Tighten that one until the sound being produced at that point on the head resembles the sound produced at the first tension rod.
5. Repeat the process on the tension rod next to the first one.
6. Repeat the process on the tension rod directly opposite that one.
7. Continue that procedure around the drum until all tension rods have been tightened to the degree desired. On a six-lug drum, the tightening pattern of the tension rods should be 1-4, 2-5, 3-6.

Overtightening heads will reduce their productivity and life span. A prescribed degree to which the tension of batter and snare heads should match each other is an issue yet to be resolved. For a brighter sound, the snare head should be somewhat tighter than the batter head. The reverse also applies. The exact choice remains that of the performer.

The alternating-tension-rod tuning process can be used with both indefinite- and definite-pitched drums. The result to be achieved for indefinite-pitched drums should be to produce a percussive sound appropriate to the type of music to be performed. Definite-pitched instruments should be tuned to the pitch indicated in the music to be played.

Some percussionists believe that snare drums of indefinite pitch should indeed be tuned to pitches. When tapping a snare drum lightly, one can hear a definite pitch. Depending on the depth of the shell and the tension of the heads, the pitches heard can range from G to B; however, these definite pitches are never heard in performance.

Those in the "pitch camp" further advise that the snare or bottom head should be tuned to sound a fourth or fifth above the pitch of the batter head. It is their contention that this highly sophisticated level of tuning a drum of indefinite pitch will provide the best level of performance for that instrument. Players can decide to what degree they wish to carry out the tuning process.

Timpani: Timpani are definite-pitched instruments and have two levels of tuning. There is a fundamental tuning where, with the pedal in the heel-down position, the heads are tuned to a particular pitch prescribed by the size of the instrument and the music to be played. The tuning process is identical to that of the snare and bass drums except that the ultimate goal is to achieve the pitch prescribed.

Tap the head lightly with a timpani mallet about four inches from the rim while turning the tension rod in the direction required to achieve the desired pitch. Again the player alternates the tension rod being turned as described above using the 1-4, 2-5, 3-6 pattern.

The following is a list of the notes to which the different-size timpani can be tuned and the approximate ascending range of notes that can be produced with the use of the pedal (as a point of reference, C4 is middle C. C2 is 2 octaves below middle C):

A 30–32-inch kettle can be tuned to C2 and pedaled up to F3.
A 28–29-inch kettle can be tuned to F3 and pedaled up to D4.
A 25–26-inch kettle can be tuned to Bb3 and pedaled up to Gb4.
A 23–24-inch kettle can be tuned to D3 and pedaled up to Bb4.
A 20–22-inch kettle can be tuned to F4 and pedaled up to D5.

The Timpani Pedal: The timpani pedal must be properly adjusted in order to hold the position set by the player. To adjust the tension of the pedal, one must proceed as follows:

1. With the head properly tuned to the fundamental tone, depress the pedal toe down to its maximum position and release the foot from the pedal. It should remain in that position.

2. If the pedal moves back on its own when the foot is released, turn the adjustment knob on the housing above the pedal to the right to tighten the tension spring.
3. Conversely, if the pedal in the heel-down position moves up on its own when the foot is released, turn the knob to the left to loosen the spring tension.
4. A properly adjusted pedal should remain at any point in its range without having to be held in place by the player's foot.

Timpani Heads: When replacing a timpano head, one will discover that the size of the diameter of the original head, when measured in inches, does not match the size of the instrument. A 26-inch drum does not use a 26-inch head. The reason for this discrepancy is that timpani heads generally need to be as much as one to two inches larger than the actual circumference of the drum in order to tune properly. To replace a timpano head, it is best to remove the original head and use it as a guide to order the new one. Timpani head charts are provided by the larger drumhead manufactures to help in selecting the proper-size head.

Summary: Percussion instruments are usually the last to receive any maintenance attention in the average school instrument inventory. It is true that by their very nature they are more durable, require fewer adjustments, and can literally withstand a beating. However, they still need attention if they are to give their best. Cleaning, adjusting, tuning, and replacing worn or broken parts are all part of the job of ensuring that the instruments in the percussion section live a long and productive life.

Conclusion

In the introduction, I stated that teaching is difficult and that teaching in the arts is even more challenging because the subject matter is abstract and not easily processed by most individuals. When reviewing the various chapters of this book, one discovers that although teaching instrumental music is indeed difficult, it is also possible to do it right. This is not an easy job, but it can be done well if the teacher is willing to take the time and effort to fully prepare for the task.

Investing in learning the information and skills required to implement the processes outlined is essential to success. Among the necessary skill sets are the many steps one must take to direct new students to the instrument on which they will most likely succeed. Concurrent with that process is administering the program, giving proper care to the school musical instrument inventory, and being well-informed about the issues involved in running the business end of a school music program. These procedures are all part of the game. They are not easy to execute, but they are wonderfully challenging, and when successfully carried out, enormously gratifying.

I wish you the very best in the adventure!

About the Author

Michael Pagliaro is certified by the New York State Department of Education as a teacher of music (grades K–12), supervisor of secondary education, and secondary school principal, and by the New York City Board of Education as teacher of orchestral music. He holds the degrees of BS in music, MA in music education, MS in school administration and supervision, and ScD in musical instrument technology. He was a professor of instrumental music and musical instrument technology at two private colleges in Westchester County, New York.

Dr. Pagliaro has devoted over six decades to teaching the technology and science of acoustical orchestral instruments to teachers, students, technicians, supervisors, and professionals in the field of music. He has filled the role of military band master, church choir director, founder of two musical instrument companies still in operation, and inventor and patent holder of four music-related products sold worldwide; he also is associate editor for the Italian Cultural Society of the Palm Beaches, has written six books, is about to complete his seventh, and has had seventeen articles on musical instruments and music in general published in various periodicals and professional house organs.

His most recent publication, *The Musical Instrument Desk Reference: An Instant Resource for the Musical Instrument General Practitioner*, published by Scarecrow Press, was written in response to requests from practitioners who, for whatever reason, are required to deal with instruments on which they are *not* proficient. Using a quick start followed by an in-depth approach, the book provides basic introductory information on woodwind, brass, non-fretted string, and percussion instruments commonly used in concert bands and orchestras. This book is now on the shelves of almost five hundred university music department research libraries in eight countries, as well as numerous public, school, and private libraries.

The String Owner's Guide, a book directed to the owners of the violin, viola, cello, and double bass, will be released by Scarecrow Press in December of 2014.